FOGGY

THE CHAMPIONSHIP YEARS

THE CHAMPIONSHIP YEARS

Carl Fogarty
with Neil Bramwell

CollinsWillow
An Imprint of HarperCollinsPublishers

First published in 2004 by
CollinsWillow
an imprint of
HarperCollins*Publishers*
London

Copyright © Carl Fogarty and Neil Bramwell 2004

9 8 7 6 5 4 3 2 1

A CIP catalogue record for this book
is available from the British Library

The HarperCollins website address is:
www.harpercollins.co.uk

ISBN 0-00-719070-0

Colour origination by Saxon Group
Printed and bound by Bath Press

All photographs supplied courtesy of Gold&Goose
Supplementary photographs provided by Kel Edge

Contents

One of the questions that I have been asked most frequently since my retirement from racing is whether team ownership can ever replace the thrill of winning a race as a rider. Well, the answer is definitely 'No!' And in this book, which focuses on my winning and the sheer emotion I felt passing that chequered flag in first place, it should be obvious for all to see. It wasn't riding at incredible speeds or getting my knee down through a corner, it was knowing I was the best. These pictures show that I was never one to hide my emotions, and how my single-mindedness might not have made me the most popular rider in the paddock while I was racing. Nowadays all the riders seem to be friends but there was usually a tension in the air when I was racing. I had to make myself almost hate my rivals so that I would be even more determined to beat them at whatever cost. And my fans loved it!

But, as they say, all good things must come to an end and, after the crash at Phillip Island in 2000, when I shattered my left shoulder, it was simply no longer possible to ride. Most sportsmen have to decide the best time to call it a day and retire – but the decision was made for me.

The question was then what the future held. Sportsmen can either disappear into the background, counting their money, or accept a new challenge. And I don't think I would ever have been happy retired from racing if I hadn't had something to focus my competitive instincts on. So, the next best thing to winning races as a rider has to be winning them as a team owner. That in itself is easier said than done because motorsport is a costly business. You cannot simply decide to set up your own team without the necessary backing. And maybe this is where my career has come full circle: for if I had not been so intent on winning when I was racing, I would not be involved in bike racing at the level I am today.

I am best known for my four World Superbike titles. Those championship wins were achieved when World Superbikes was at its peak, with a lot of factory-supported teams and a lot of very talented riders. And it wasn't as easy for the Ducati factory riders in those days as it has been recently. Believe me, I fully earned every race win and every world championship. But people sometimes forget that I have another three world titles under my belt, two in Formula One TT racing and one World Endurance Championship. Add to that the FIM World Cup title in 1990 and I have won eight world titles in total.

Having been brought up around road racing – my dad George was also a racer – I knew from an early age that all I wanted to do in life was to become the world champion. But those early days, when we operated out of the back of a van with minimum sponsorship, were a far cry from the level of support that the top teams now receive. Just look at the pictures from Pergusa in 1988 to get a feel for the kind of outfit that was behind me back in those days.

But everyone has to start somewhere and, from my days in schoolboy motocross through to my holding those world championship trophies aloft, one thread ran through my career – I could not stand to lose. And that was probably what set me apart from other riders. It didn't matter what the race, there was only one place to finish. And, before I became a factory rider, I needed to race and win as often as possible just to pay the bills.

So, as a privateer in 1992, I jumped at the chance to ride in the Malaysian championships for the PETRONAS Sprinta team, run by David Wong, a consultant for the PETRONAS Motorsport department. There were a couple of fast young Aussies to beat, but I managed to win a few races quite comfortably. That must have impressed PETRONAS, Malaysia's state-owned petroleum corporation, because when we started to look for sponsorship for my own team in 2001, David, who had remained in touch throughout my career, was soon in contact. PETRONAS had been funding the development of a new 989cc triple engine, called the GP1, with its Swiss-based joint-venture company Sauber PETRONAS Engineering. It was expected that the engine would be leased to Grand Prix motorcycle teams, but my successful association with PETRONAS resulted in a five-year World Superbikes project, with my team – Foggy PETRONAS Racing – making our debut in 2003 on the first Malaysian superbike, the PETRONAS FP1.

The sheer scale of the project, which also involved the creation of an elite race bike for the road, really hit home when the road version was launched at the PETRONAS twin towers in Kuala Lumpur in November 2003. Sure, we had a few teething troubles in the first year of racing but, at the time of going to press, we have achieved two podiums and a pole position, with promising signs of more to come. But, as everyone should know by now, I won't be happy until one of our riders is standing on the top step of that podium.

You might well ask what Carl Fogarty, a lad from Blackburn, Lancashire, who didn't pay much attention at school but was pretty talented on a motorbike, can bring to the running of a successful racing team. Well, I pretty much leave the business side of things to the experts. And, sure, my reputation helps raise the profile of the team, which is also very important. But with that reputation comes expectation – and nobody's expectations are higher than my own. Throughout my career as a rider I would never settle for second best. I expected to win races and I expect my team to do the same. When Chris Walker, another competitive guy if ever there was one, brought the bike home in third place at Valencia in the first race of the 2004 season, I couldn't help leaping over the pitwall and onto the track to celebrate. If just a fraction of that desire for success can rub off on the team, from the riders down throughout the whole team, then I will feel I have been successful in my new role.

So, while I am able to look back on the championship years with pride, I'd like to think that there are more chapters of this book still to fill…

Formula

One TT

1988

Ulster

My first ever world championship win! This was a big race for the Dunlop brothers, Joey and Robert, in front of a massive crowd of 60,000 at the fast but dangerous Dundrod circuit. It was very narrow in places and people were extremely close to the action when sitting on the banking. Bad weather was almost guaranteed, making it even more dangerous. The event was a journey into the unknown for me and it showed when I qualified on the fifth row in 21st. But I shot through the field like a scalded cat and, by the end of the first lap, I was in the lead. I was very fast in the wet in those days and the Metzeler tyres worked well in the rain. I led until the finish, expecting Joey to come past at any moment. But Joey only managed seventh and suddenly, out of nowhere, I was five and a half points behind the leader of the world championship with just two rounds remaining, and I eventually won by 16 seconds. Michaela, having tuned the radio to an Irish station, was listening to events from a car park in Bolton.

You can see the straw bales giving minimal protection from the road signs. You also get an impression of how big the RC30 was – it was basically a road bike with a Tony Scott-tuned engine.

Pergusa

A whole squad of guys from Blackburn – I nicknamed them the Ant Hill Mob after the Whacky Races cartoon characters – had travelled down to Sicily, some in the back of the van and a few more in an old Jaguar owned by the guy who ran the local nightclub, to support me. Early in the race I was battling with an Italian on a factory Bimota, Gianluca Galasso, but when he broke down I was out on my own.

You could just about do the race on one full tank but, with just a few more miles left to complete, the bike started to cut out. So I dived into the pit-lane and the crowd went ballistic as this suddenly made the race much more interesting. Needless to say, the Ant Hill Mob weren't ready so we just poured the petrol – just enough so that I could make the final lap. I shouted at them to push me back out and luckily I made it round and won the race. That left me at the top of the world championship standings with one round remaining at Donington – and fifth place there was enough to win my first world championship.

I don't know where Joey Dunlop popped up from. Earlier that weekend my mates had to take him to hospital after he crashed in qualifying.

My mechanic Lou Durkin,
in the best pit-lane attire,
frantically pushing me back out for that final lap

Pergusa

The day was red hot and I was sweating like a racehorse on the podium. I was not even wearing a vest under my leathers it was so hot. All I needed to do now was keep an eye out for the Mafia after beating the local favourite!

Punching the air as I crossed the line.

Assen

This was my first win of many at this circuit. The race lasted around 30 laps and we had to come in for a pit-stop to re-fuel. This was nothing like Formula One car pit-stops but we did have a quick-filler, which could half-fill the tank in around 10 seconds. (One of my mates kept it as a souvenir.) The race was during Grand Prix weekend, so there was a massive crowd at the circuit. I was riding an RC30, semi-supported by Honda UK, and sponsored by Appleby Glade. At the time Steve Hislop was leading the championship, having won in the Isle of Man after the opening round in Japan. The race was an absolute cruise after qualifying on pole.

With this many Brits taking part, it looks more like a British championship race. I had just gone underneath Roger Burnett (51) and was about to clear off and didn't see anyone for the rest of the race. You can see Trevor Nation on the Norton, followed by a glimpse of Hislop's helmet, then James Whitham and Anders Andersson (5).

Kouvola

This was a strange circuit, set in an industrial estate where nearly every corner was a right angle, although the Finnish crowds were really enthusiastic. The key to a good lap, and to staying on the bike, was dodging the manhole covers in the middle of the road. It was actually pretty safe, as the industrial units themselves were behind a kind of ditch, but you would never catch me going round there now! I was much quicker than the other guys, including a quick Finnish rider called Jari Suhonen, and easily qualified on pole. I was now leading the world championship and had only to turn up in Ulster and finish in the top six to clinch my second world title…

The champagne must have been disgusting as we all spit it out after taking a swig.

FIM World

Cup

Isle of Man

Isle of Man

This was my first major TT win and the first time that I had my hands on one of their massive trophies. When I won the production race in 1989, I had been gutted when the trophy I was presented with was much smaller. I also won the Senior race this year but it was the F1 win which counted as a world title victory, albeit in the newly invented FIM World Cup. The series had lost world championship status due to a lack of the required minimum number of races. I was team-mate with Steve Hislop (who was tragically killed in a helicopter crash in 2003) for Honda Britain. He had been getting all the attention for his achievements the previous year, when he won three races at the TT, including reaching a new record average speed of 120mph. I had to make myself hate him so I could beat him, especially as I was worried by the muscle I had pulled in my arm during practice. Riders set off at 10-second intervals and I was 20 seconds behind Steve, which unnerved him. I had caught up with him by the second lap and, going into the tight right-hand Sulby Bridge corner, we both braked way too late. I managed to get round the corner but Steve ran straight on and retired on the next lap, claiming there was a problem with his brakes. Then all I had to do was cruise around for the next five laps.

Getting down to business, exiting
Quarter Bridge on the first lap.

Exiting Brabham Bridge corner,
pulling the RC30 hard away from
the kerb.

I am either squinting
because the sun is in
my eyes or because
I am so fired up.

A tradition at the Isle of Man was to line the first three bikes up – myself, Nick Jeffries and Robert Dunlop.

Another lesson in how not to wear a winner's cap

Isle of Man

Macau GP

Jamie Whitham and I were invited out to the Macau Grand Prix, not part of the official GP world championship, to ride Yamahas. It was a two-legged race and I did all the hard work in the first leg. Jamie and local star Toshihiko Honma, who had both competed there before, were swapping the lead in the early stages while I sat behind collecting a set of dead flies on my visor. Once past those two, and after narrowly missing Jamie who had tried to out-brake me and had bounced back into the track after crashing into the straw bales, I had a clear run. The track was really bumpy and it was a dangerously tight street circuit, but I set the fastest lap of the race and built up something like an eight-second lead from that first leg. In the second leg the bike cut out whenever we were on a section of the track coming back down to sea level, so it must have been running rich. We all came to the finish together and, although I had finished third in that leg, I was comfortably overall winner. So technically that makes me the only rider to win a World Superbike race, a Formula One TT, a World Endurance race and a GP!

I can't remember exactly what I said to Jamie out of the side of my mouth, probably something about a girl in the crowd, but he obviously found it funny! I have still got that set of leathers.

World

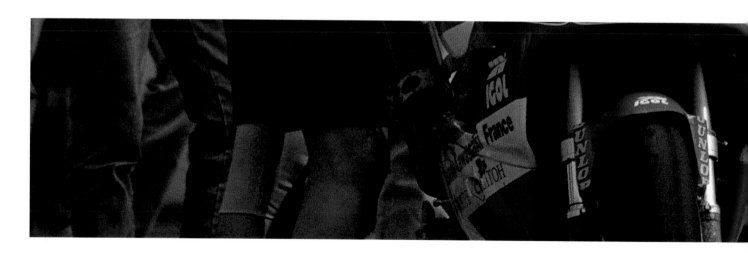

Endurance

Le Mans

This was my first 24-hour race so I was a bit wet behind the ears.
My team-mates were Terry Rymer and a Belgian, Michel Simeon.
My first mistake was forgetting to hit the start button after sprinting across
the track for the start, so I was left for dead. But I managed to claw my
way back to second, behind the other Kawasaki France team of Alex Vieira
in the first 50-minute session. The next mistake was tucking into the
hospitality food during my breaks, so I felt sick throughout the race.
And the third error was to fall asleep, which left me feeling crap when a
mechanic woke me up with the warning that it would be my turn in
10 laps. I have a lazy eye at the best of times but, just waking up, it was
even worse and I nearly fell off twice in the first couple of laps.

The other Kawasaki team had snapped a cam-chain and broken down and our
bosses were worried that the same might happen to us. So our mechanics
incited the crowd to invade the track as there was an hour still remaining
and the officials had no option but to call an early end to the race.

This is late on in the race, when we were leading. I had changed leathers to
let my Kawasaki set dry out. The bike was always bottoming out, as can be
seen from the scratches on the fairing.

Le Mans

Me, Simeon and Rymer
(right) being mobbed by
our mechanics. It was fantastic
to have won my first 24-hour race

Spa

This race was a real battle. I had qualified on pole and, along with Terry Rymer, had Jehan d'Orgeix in our team. The Suzuki team was always less than a minute behind and kept pegging us back during pit stops until they crashed out on oil – something that led to my scariest incident in racing. I was in agony anyway as I had leaned over too far in a corner and caught my finger on one of the poles that carry the reflector strips for night riding, cracking a bone. Then one of my mechanics pulled the nozzle out of the fuel tank and nearly blinded me by spraying petrol into my eyes. I almost had to let d'Orgeix back out but he was our slowest rider and I dragged him off the bike at the last minute. During that session I felt the bike starting to slide at the fast Blanchimont corner. Suzuki rider Herve Moineau had crashed out and dumped oil on the track and I had hit it. If the bike had gone from under me I would have slid straight into the ambulance that was treating him and I would definitely have died. But somehow I managed to stay on and to this day believe that I cheated death there.

Taking the lead at the bus-stop chicane on this beautiful circuit.
I think it is still a favourite with the F1 drivers as it is so big and flowing.

Despite this slow start – I am number 2 – I am sure I was leading
by the end of the first lap. Steve Hislop (1) qualified in third.

Spa

Hislop is right behind after I slowed
right down when it started to rain
before going to change tyres.

You can just see the boot of Terry Rymer who is waiting to get on after my stop. The rider is not allowed to get off the bike until the bike has been re-fuelled

Bol D'Or

This wasn't the last round of the championship, but it was the last 24-hour race as the next two were intended to be 8-hour. For this round Steve Hislop was our third rider, so we were definitely favourites to follow up our first two wins. I qualified on pole, and it was always a great feeling to beat your team-mates – not to mention getting the £1000 bonus (quite a lot in those days). I took the lead going into the last corner of the first lap so we led every single lap of the race. Steve was faster during the night than he was during the day, which was amazing. I couldn't see a thing during the night! We won easily and my only problem that weekend was a £100 fine for 'accidentally' running a French marshal over in my car in the paddock!

Coming round the last tight right-hand corner at Bol D'Or.

Hanging off the bike as best I could while coming round the
final corner. These were effectively full F1 bikes and were

It wasn't often that I limbered up before a race but maybe I was more conscious of it before a 24-hour race.

The Suzuki is behind me coming onto the start-finish straight on the second lap.

I am wearing the red armband of the number one rider as we acknowledge the crowd on our victory lap.

Bol D'Or

Phillip Island

We hadn't actually planned to do this race but, despite victory in the first three rounds, the championship was not yet secure. I had qualified on pole but, almost as soon as we set off, it started to rain. It was the coldest I have ever been and the race was cut down from eight to six hours. Something like 20 marshals had to be taken to hospital with hypothermia. I remember not even taking my helmet off when handing over to Rymer because it was so cold. But the weather was the only competition that we faced. The fact that our main rival Michele Graziano had come third meant that Terry and I had become world champions. Then I had to go out and do a World Superbike round the next day!

It is difficult to say what time of day this was taken because it was pretty much dark all day long. I am just getting onto the bike while the front wheel is being changed.

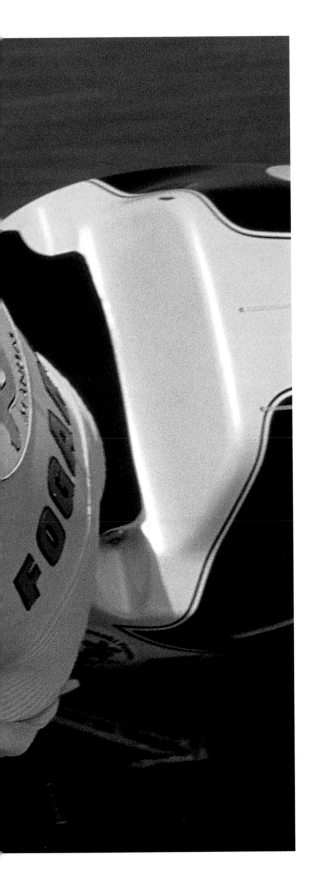

Johor

The pressure was off in some ways but I still had one thing on my mind. Terry and I went into this race with exactly the same points. I had already pulled out of the second World Superbike race in Australia the previous week when it started to drizzle, claiming there was a technical problem because I did not want to get injured and risk missing the Johor race, as then Terry would have been world champion on his own. I was equally cautious qualifying in Malaysia. But, when the race started, I knew I was going to finish with just as many points, so I could relax. I still managed to qualify on pole and we led from start to finish, lapping the rest of the other teams.

From the shadows you can tell the sun is directly overhead, creating stinking-hot conditions.

World

Superbikes

Donington

Nobody was more surprised than I was at my first ever World Superbikes win. I had had to buy my own bike and truck as a privateer that year – a big gamble but one that paid off. It was the first time I had been on the Ducati 888 for three consecutive dry days but I managed to get onto pole without too much difficulty. It was only then that I started to think that I had a chance of winning: the bike was doing everything I wanted – so much so that I was going through the chicanes and hairpin in second gear, something I never did any other year. I led the first race by two or three seconds before sliding off at Goddards – a pathetically slow crash. I was so angry with myself, especially after all the disappointments of the previous year. I was at a real low. I then got a really bad start for the second race but picked the rest off, one by one, managing to come through the field and win, despite a scare late on when my bike started to jump out of gear. I was too emotional for the usual celebrations and just slumped over my tank, the tears rolling down my face, punching the air with my fist all the way round the track.

Negotiating Goddard's during my first World Superbike win.

Albacete

This round saw my first two wins as a factory Ducati rider on the 888, following my first World Superbike win at Donington the previous year. Raymond Roche, my team manager, told me to use four gears instead of six, with the first gear as long as possible, as this circuit was a bit like a go-kart track. It did the trick. As a factory rider, I felt the pressure to perform even more so when, while on the grid, Michaela said, 'You can win this'. I got away first in both races, controlling them both.

Going into a tight right hairpin with Stephane Mertens right behind me. He fell off at that corner and was narrowly missed by Aaron Slight.

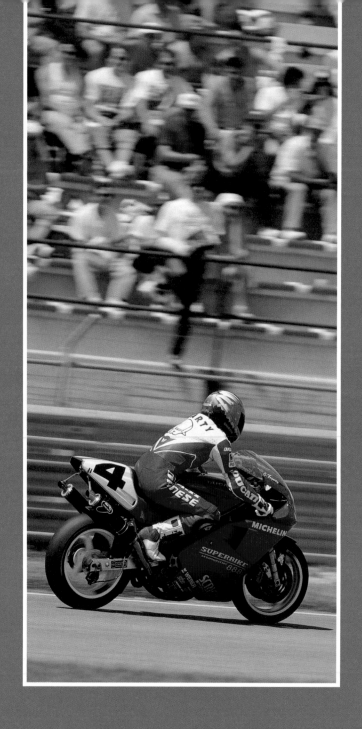

Hard on the
brakes, just about
to peel into turn one

Sharing a joke with Aaron Slight, which was one of the few times we were actually talking, although we actually got on quite well that year. As our reputations and pay packets grew, we became less friendly. My attitude to other riders didn't leave me with a lot of mates – but it did win races.

This shot was taken in practice after winning the North West 200 a couple of weeks earlier, as I always wore my lucky green vest from the NW 200 on race days, from that meeting onward.

Albacete

Brno

This was another beautiful circuit – one of the best in Europe – with a long lap of over two minutes. I went into the sixth round fourth in the championship and 25.5 points behind my team-mate Giancarlo Falappa. I had a good battle with Scott Russell in the early stages of the first race after qualifying on pole but I pulled away and won the first race comfortably. I was leading the second race as well but the bike lost power, so I had to nurse it home before it shat itself as it crossed the line. This was one of the many mishaps that year that eventually cost me the title. Without them, I would probably have had nine wins in a row as I was now on a roll. However, Falappa had crashed out of the second race too so I was now second in the championship, 19 points behind Russell.

The trophies we were presented with had no plaque to signify that they were first place but the trophies for the winners were way bigger than those for the runners-up. So, rather than have a poxy one next to the big one in our trophy cabinets, Russell and I decided to flip a coin for who took both big ones home, as we had each come first and second that weekend. The saying goes, tails never fails. But it did this time and the bastard got to keep both.

Battling with Russell early on in the first race, although I have run a bit wide.

Anderstorp

I liked this circuit, which was very open with a massive straight – it used to be an air force base. The corners were also banked, which suited my style. I had only raced there a couple of times before, when I was sixth in a Grand Prix and when I had achieved my best World Superbike result in 1991 on the Honda. I was probably on the best bike out there and Russell was already complaining that the Ducati was faster out of the corners than his four-cylinder Kawasaki, which was faster down the straights – but this was a long straight! His face was a picture on the podium and our war of words kicked off when I described it as looking like a 'slapped arse'!

The story of both races was simple: I got in front early on and gradually pulled away to win comfortably.

Negotiating the left-hand final corner before entering start-finish. The long hair coming from underneath my helmet was Michaela's fault.

Slight follows me
around in practice,
when it must have rained.

A good action shot
around one of the tighter
left-handers at Anderstorp leading

onto the make-shift start-finish straight

Anderstorp

Johor

This was another double win in the unbearable heat of Malaysia. The track was a bit rough in places and this was to be the last World Superbike race held there, although there was a Grand Prix there later on. I knew the circuit from when I raced there in the Malaysian Superbike championship for the PETRONAS Sprinta team – an association which was to become much stronger later on in my career when they sponsored my Foggy PETRONAS Racing team from 2002 onwards.

The first race was very comfortable but Russell had a knack of making the right changes for the second race and challenging me a lot harder. It was one of the toughest races I have ever had and he pushed me all the way until I pulled a 1.5 second gap with two laps remaining. Words can't describe how pleased I was to see that pit board. At the end of the race I had just enough energy to punch the air all the way around the lap of honour. The points difference between me and Russell was now down to just five!

The damp towel around the shoulder is an indication of just how hot it was.

Waiting for the green light under the burning tropical sun

Trying hard to put some distance between Russell and myself in the second race.

I am leading Russell in the second race. I hate to think how that marshal would have reacted if there had been an accident in front of him as he doesn't look too interested.

Johor

Sugo

This should have been another double victory. Usually the main threat here at quite a technical and difficult circuit, without too much grip, is the fast Japanese wild card riders. This time the problem was a slow local back marker. I had qualified on pole and won the first race quite comfortably to lead the world championship for the only time that season. In the second race Russell must have been a bit embarrassed that two other Kawasaki wild cards had beaten him in the first so as usual he was pushing me harder. I had just created a bit of daylight between us, about two seconds with three laps remaining, when I got held up by the guy I was about to lap. I tried to go underneath him in the second part of the tight double apex right-hander turn one. But I must have been on the gas too early as I had a massive high-side and landed on my coccyx. Ouch! It was just another incident that was to eventually cost me the title. While I continued to win races and then not finish, Russell always seemed to be picking up points. My team boss Raymond Roche then tried to kill the Japanese rider who caused the crash.

The poor girl – I think she was our interpreter –
was getting a proper soaking.

Assen

It was all getting a bit familiar at Assen: pole position and another double win. But Russell was second in both races and, under the old points system, I was still seven points behind him in the championship. Each round was now following the familiar format. I won the first race by a mile and then he made improvements to push me harder in the second. However, he could only stay with me at Assen for a few laps before I pulled away again. At that point I had won ten races in the championship, with Russell having won just three. It just shows the value of consistency.

In full flow at my favourite circuit.

Michaela does not look too impressed as she holds the brolly on her own, while I probably share a dirty joke with Raymond Roche and Slick. I always seemed to be more relaxed at Assen.

Top right: Slight is almost touching my back wheel during the first lap action.

Bottom right:
Celebrating on my victory lap.

Assen

Standing on the pegs as I return to the pit-lane to celebrate the double win with a flag tied around my neck.

Estoril

I missed the opportunity here to capitalize on Russell's bad luck when he broke down during the first race as I had already crashed out. There were a lot of wet patches on the track and I hit one and went down. I would only have been about 12 points behind him with three races remaining if I had stayed on and won that race. Still, I made up for it in race two and Ducati received a few complaints when my hand gestures to Russell went out on live television. As it turned out I would not have had the chance to close the gap in the final round, as the races were cancelled when the riders protested that the track was too dangerous in Mexico.

Trying to stay on my feet as the bike hurtles through the gravel.

Donington

I had already been at the circuit that year, to debut the 916 in the British championship, where I won both races to the obvious delight of the Castiglioni brothers who owned Ducati. But the bike didn't feel ready for the world stage and I moaned that I wanted last year's bike back. It felt nervous and twitchy and the fact that I won the first race only shocked me. I was really struggling to get the power down in mid-corner. This was also the first time I had come across Troy Corser, who was leading at one point, along with Fabrizio Pirovano. I came third in the second race behind Russell, which was really where I had expected to come in the first race.

Coming out of the final corner, leading Falappa, Russell, Corser and Pirovano.

Peeling into **Coppice** before coming onto the back straight. **This shot was taken during practice because Bontempi is close behind me. He was the worst rider for trying to get a tow from someone so as to record a fast qualifying lap.**

Donington

Preparing to get into the back of the control car waving to the crowd after the first race. The big red mark on my forehead is testament to the fact that I always seemed to wear a tighter-fitting helmet than most riders

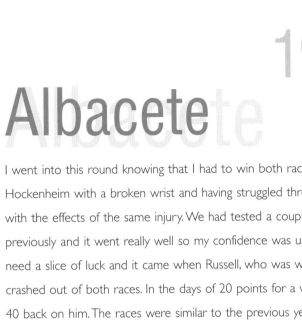

Albacete

I went into this round knowing that I had to win both races, having missed Hockenheim with a broken wrist and having struggled through Misano with the effects of the same injury. We had tested a couple of days previously and it went really well so my confidence was up. But you always need a slice of luck and it came when Russell, who was way ahead, crashed out of both races. In the days of 20 points for a win, I had pulled 40 back on him. The races were similar to the previous year as I controlled them from start to finish.

This is in the very early stages of the race, trying to put some distance between the chasing pack and myself.

How Cool Am I?

At the time I thought this picture, taken for a magazine, was the best I had ever had taken. Now I think I looked too weird without my goatee, even though I did have more chains than 50 Cent! You can see Ernest Ribe-Barber, the well-known wheelchair-bound Spanish journalist reflected in my sunglasses

Albacete

I got the whole-shot in the first race, with Piergiorgio Bontempi behind me. He was good at Albacete but crap everywhere else

Left: This was a pre-publicity shot for the British GP, taken in Spain. I was meant to be indicating that I was going to beat up Kevin Schwantz and Mick Doohan. But as it happened I didn't race because the fuel injection system of the Cagiva threw me off the bike during practice.

Middle: This picture was used on the front cover of MCN.

Right: Returning to the pit-lane, saluting my team.

Zeltweg

I went into this round on the back of two wins so confidence was high. The circuit was later changed to make it slower, with a couple of really sharp hairpins, but I much preferred this faster lay-out. I still managed to qualify in pole position, winning my weight in Austrian wine in the process. I had to go and sit on some scales to be weighed, as they piled the wine on the other scale. But I was not in the mood – I just wanted to go back to the motorhome to sleep. So I stuck my toe under the carpet so that they had to give me much more wine than I actually weighed. But it was disgusting (I found a bottle in the kitchen ten years later – and it hadn't improved with age).

I won both races comfortably on one of my best days ever in racing. What made it better was that it was the day of the Brazil versus Italy World Cup football final in the States, so I spent the whole weekend supporting Brazil in order to wind my Italian mechanics up.

Hanging off the bike through a tight right-hander. The dark visor was like looking through an oil slick.

Gary Dickinson, who was best man at my wedding, pushes me back to the garage after breaking down during practice

Doing some more homework in my motorhome with James, this time reading some 'bike' magazines. Obviously Michaela and Andrea were elsewhere.

Zeltweg

Sentul

I already had something to celebrate arriving in Indonesia as Michaela had
just given birth to our second daughter, Claudia. And I should have
celebrated with another double win as I was leading the first race by seven
seconds with seven laps remaining when the Ducati broke down due to
a problem they were having with the supply of crank casings. I was gutted,
as we had suffered more than our fair share of reliability problems that
year. And I was desperate to get back to winning ways after Honda had
won an appeal and Slight had been re-awarded points he had been
docked at Donington for using an illegal fuel. There was now genuine bad
feeling between the Ducati and Honda camps. But normal service was
resumed when I cleared off in the second race to win by a mile. Jamie
Whitham had won the first race and we had a laugh by firing cake made
for the special ceremony at the compere's back!

Ready for the start of the race.

Assen

Turned up, won two races, went home! It was well established that this was my favourite circuit but now the pressure was on to win both races in order to claw the points gap back with Russell, having just lost two races in Japan and Indonesia through bad luck. But my bikes always seemed to do what I wanted them to at Assen. I never had any problems trying to get them to turn into corners, or hold their line. Maybe the camber of the corners helped, but I never suffered chatter or suspension problems there either. Once I got into the lead in both races there was no looking back, and no serious challenge. The only thing I had to worry about was whether the good weather would hold, as it threatened to rain all weekend.

I am leaning over, celebrating, with the Union Jack tied round my neck.

After having qualified in the wet, I am joined on the front row by some unlikely candidates: Lucchiari, Terry Rymer and Paolo Casoli.

This shows how much corner speed I would carry into the bends and how comfortable I look mid-corner.

Slight looks knackered
after the second race

Assen

San Marino (Mugello)

I entered this round leading the championship by 11 points from Slight and 15 from Scott Russell, as the FIM had made a final decision that Slight was to lose the 17 points from Donington. I qualified on pole and there wasn't much I could do to beat Russell in the first race, as he was faster than I was there. I would gain in some parts of this big circuit, and he would pull away in others. It was his turn for some bad luck in the second race when he broke down when leading again. It reversed what had happened in Indonesia and put me into a strong position going into the penultimate round at Donington. Little did I know then that I would leave there with a lead of just five points.

On pole on the start line.

Phillip Island

The pressure was on: going into this round just five points ahead of Russell but, for once, I decided to let him do all the talking while I concentrated on the job in hand. I qualified second fastest but knew that I had been held up by two slow riders on my flying qualifying lap. I got in front early on and led the race, although Russell did come past at one point.

It didn't worry me; as I knew that I was so much faster than him from Siberia to the last corner. So I came back past him straight away, got my head down and pulled away to win the race comfortably. Anthony Gobert, under team orders, had to slow down and let Russell finish second and, even though I knew I only had to finish in the top four in race two, it was a nerve-wracking wait until the afternoon race. I remember sitting in the circuit café with James Whitham, when Barry Sheene came in to wish me the best of luck, telling me he realized what I must be going through.

I didn't get the best of starts for the second race but having worked my way through the field, I decided against all my instincts not to mix it with Russell and his wild team-mate Gobert. So I just sat in behind Russell in third and he hated it. With three laps to go he gestured as though he had thrown in the towel and, although I didn't trust him at first, he did pull in on the next lap. All I had to do was to stay upright and win my first World Superbike title. After such a traumatic year, my emotions got the better of me and I cried all the way into the pits when I headed straight into the waiting arms of Michaela.

A proud moment as my achievement starts to sink in.

The battle for the world title
on the starting line at Phillip Island

Phillip Island

The view that the rest of the riders had 'enjoyed' for most of the season!

Slick holds out the board indicating that I had won my first World Superbike title. I don't remember seeing it, but I do remember the chequered flag.

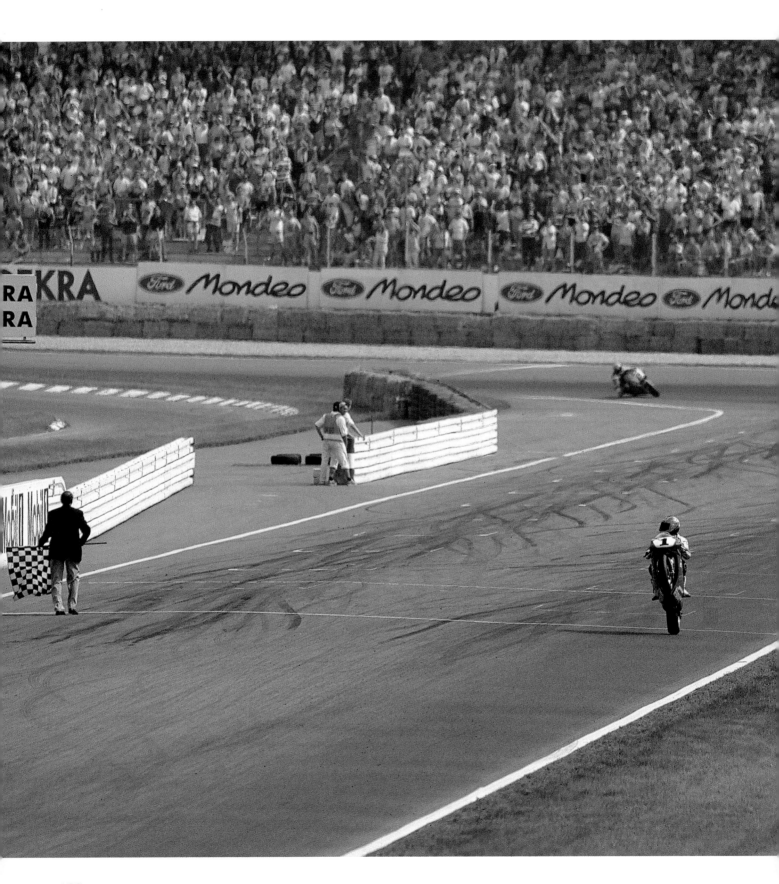

Hockenheim

My first race as defending World Superbike champion, and what better way to start off than by winning both races? And the easiest way to win them was by clearing off at the start – something difficult to do at Hockenheim. The improvements to the 916 over the winter had worked wonders. The suspension had been changed at the front and rear and the engine was a lot smoother. This round provided my first win in Germany and, fittingly enough, it was on VE Day. This was really the first year that the national newspapers started sitting up and taking notice, especially *The Sun*, who asked me to strike Churchill's V-sign pose after the races.

What a great picture! Looking over towards pitwall as I pull a wheelie in front of a massive crowd, the rest of the riders only just coming round the final corner.

It looks as though the bike is going away from me and, from my body language, this shot might have been taken during qualifying as I do not seem to be trying too hard.

Dragging the freight train behind me before eventually breaking them up.

Having a look at my back wheel as I pass the pit-lane, probably just to wind my team up so they'd start worrying that there was a problem

Hockenheim

Donington

After two seconds in Misano I was already leading the championship by 31 points and, as ever, desperate to do well in front of my fans from home. The highlight of the first race was out-braking Russell at the hairpin and then giving him the 'finger'. That was his last round in World Superbikes as he went on to Grand Prix racing with Lucky Strike Suzuki after Kevin Schwantz was injured.

The second race was much closer and I was really struggling to shake Corser off until his rear sprocket sheared off, leaving me to cruise round to victory.

I found this flag, given to me after the second race, a few years later when I moved house. It had Blackburn Rovers, my favourite football team, written across it; the guy who gave it to me was called Jake Shaw.

Starting to create
some daylight between

myself and the chasing pack early on

Troy is peeling into the left while I have flicked the bike over to the right, going through the chicane.

Donington

Going into Redgate at the start of the second lap after qualifying in pole position, and completing a perfect weekend.

San Marino (Monza)

The San Marino round is now staged at Misano but in 1995 it was at Monza. Honda had been moaning to the organizers that Ducati were at too much of an advantage so the rules were changed for this round, making us add more weight. I was under instructions from team boss Virginio Ferrari to say that the extra weight had caused difficulties but it actually worked in our favour, as I was not afraid to say after easily winning the first race. The extra weight had cured a front-end chatter problem. And the Hondas were still faster through the speed traps, as they were all year. They just couldn't manage to get the whole package together – too much power, not enough package. I was leading the second race and had just pulled away at the start of the last lap when the engine blew, leaving me with no option but to nurse the bike home in second place. I think this was the only time that engine failure had stopped me from doing a double.

This was Chili's first win, so it came accompanied by his usual hugs and kisses and uncontrollable emotions.

I am so close to Chili that it looks as though I am sitting on the back of his bike. His was not a factory bike but as fast as mine at top speed.

Albacete

I had a record to maintain here, as I had done the double in 1993 and 1994. But I only managed to win the second race this year. I spent the whole of the first race trying to get past Aaron Slight, as his bike was so quick coming out of the corners that he would pull away between bends. He was actually holding me up through the corners but I just couldn't manage to beat him on the brakes, as he was a very late braker.

The second race was a different story as I got to the front first and cleared off. 'Normal service has been resumed,' I later told the press. But I needed everyone to know just how fast the Hondas actually were and so predicted that they would be faster than the Ducati at the next round, in Austria. Slight grabbed the mike off me at the press conference and said something like 'That's right, I'll just wobble round the corners and blast away down the straight.' Then he stormed out.

It's obvious how much I hated waiting for the green light to start the races. I can't tell if the brolly girl is eyeing me up, or Michaela, or both of us. But I think it's me!

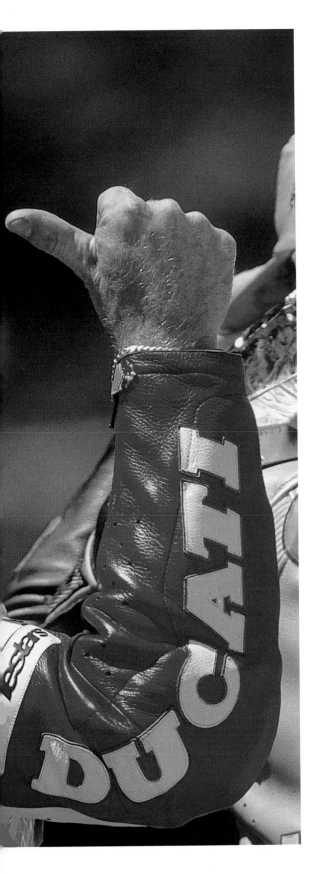

Salzburgring

This was the only time we raced at this circuit but it sticks in my memory for two reasons. Firstly, I was presented with the biggest ever trophy for winning the race, the 100th win for Ducati. Secondly, there was a massive brawl in pit-lane between the marshals and the Ducati team! It was a fast circuit, with plenty of slip-streaming, so the key was to get away from the pack, which I managed to do in the first race.

I knew that someone would then try to stick with me in the second race and, sure enough, Troy was very difficult to shake off. We were slip-streaming each other on every lap but I had sussed out where I needed to be to win the race, drifting past him up the hill. However, a back marker got in the way, I hesitated and the gap was just too much to pull back.

Don't look back in anger —
not when I have won anyway.

It looks like someone
made this flag out of
a local tree.

You can see how

focused I am as I lead Corser

Salzburgring

Brands Hatch

If I were to pick my best-ever racing weekend, this is the one that sticks in my mind. The weather was hot and the crowd bigger than it had ever been at Brands before. At that stage, I wasn't sure whether I liked the circuit and I came into the round on the back of my worst result of the season at Laguna. And Brands is very similar to Laguna in many respects. But, from the first practice session to the end of the second race, I was riding on rails. You can never complain when you leave a round with pole position, the lap record and two race wins. If anyone had closed in on me in either race I knew that I could easily have upped the pace even further – but no-one came close. For those few months I was definitely at my peak as a racer. But I did not feel in peak condition driving back to Blackburn on Monday morning with the hangover from hell.

As I came out of the last corner, the crowd were going ballistic, although they were waving Union Jacks and not the St George Cross! But what is that Aussie flag doing there?

Coming out of Druids on the opening lap of the first race

Arms aloft in celebration of the wins.

Raising one
finger, to indicate
that I'm number one

The quietest spot on the track, but only about 100 yards from the rest of civilization.

Brands Hatch

Sugo

After the double win at Brands, this win in Japan proved that I was riding at my absolute peak. After taking the lead in the first race, I had a massive crash coming out of the double apex first corner. I got on the gas that little bit too early on a track where there is very little grip anyway. The back slid right round and I thought it would just slide out. But it fired me back violently from a crazy angle and launched me into the sky. I went so far up that it looked like I was walking on air. I had just enough time to think 'Don't come down flat-footed', so I landed on my side but was still pretty knocked about.

I was given some injections before the second race and it was only afterwards that I found I had chipped bones in my hand and foot. I remember feeling terrible on the sighting lap. But, from pole, I got to a flying start before Nagai came up on my inside and nearly took me out. That wound me up and we bashed fairings a couple of times before I pulled away – but not before giving him the finger. When the adrenaline wore off towards the end of the race, when I was sure of winning, I started feeling bad again and almost passed out. But I made it and it was without doubt one of my most memorable wins.

Coming up on the inside of Aaron Slight, going into the double apex right-hand first corner.

Assen

All I really needed to do was to turn up to win my second world title, as I had almost clinched it at the previous round in Japan. Mathematically, all I had to do was finish in the points in the first race, but that didn't stop me wanting to win both. And I did, despite still feeling pretty sore from the crash at Sugo. I led the first race from start to finish, despite early pressure from Simon Crafar on the Honda. I was initially in two minds as to how to tackle the race, as I didn't need to beat him. But I tried to forget about the championship and eventually pulled away to win by around three seconds to clinch the title. So all the pressure was off for the second race and I pulled away again to win by a mile.

But the shine was taken off what should have been a great day when Pirovano's engine blew and Nagai hit the oil. At that point of the track, a safe corner, Nagai would normally just have slid off but the bike dug in, landed heavily on him and he was killed. So the race was stopped early while I was in the lead, and celebrations proved somewhat subdued.

Celebrating the world title, with Claudia, who had just turned one, and my dad and mum. I've no idea who the young lad is.

This was the first time Ducati had carried sponsorship for Kremlyovskaya Vodka, although it ran throughout 1996. It was great exposure for them at that race though their advertising looked horrible on the bike.

Michaela hugs the nearest person, who just happens to be the Ducati truck driver.

Leading Crafar through the chicane on the way to winning the world title.

Assen

Sentul

To be honest, I couldn't really be bothered going to Indonesia for the penultimate round. My head was spinning with what to do for the following year. At that stage, I still had an option to ride for Kenny Roberts' Marlboro team in the Grand Prix series. But there were also offers on the table from Ducati, Yamaha, Suzuki and Honda, and I was struggling to make up my mind. Faxes came through to my hotel in Jakarta from Chuck Askland, Roberts' team manager, but Marlboro pulled the plug because they were not interested in having a British rider. In the end, because of all the internal politics, I decided to go with the professionalism of Honda, knowing that their bike had been quick this year and might well be even faster for 1996.

At Sentul, a track similar to Monza with fast straights and a few chicanes, I won the first race very comfortably and was leading the second race when a breather pipe problem caused the bike to cut out. I pulled in immediately, my first and only breakdown of the year.

Coming out of the garage during practice and after one of Indonesia's famous tropical downpours. I needed to test the conditions in case it was wet on race day.

Hockenheim

I went into this race at an all-time low, having had a terrible start to my first season as a factory rider away from Ducati. That start had included finishing ninth and seventh in the previous round – in front of my own fans at Donington. I could not seem to get any mid-corner grip from the Honda and the rear end came round on me every time I tried to go faster. To cap it all, my trusted mechanic Slick had just been sacked and to make matters worse I had a massive crash, while going through the first chicane during practice. Nobody from the team even bothered to come and see how I was doing in the medical centre.

But I managed to get my head together and come up with a plan, which was to raise the back of the bike to help me steer quicker, hold my line better and cure the tyre chatter. In race two I managed to get a good start and was away with the leaders for the first time that season. And as the race went on, I grew in confidence and realized that I was exiting the last chicane side by side with Slight. The race was going to be won on the brakes. I just needed to be in the right place at the right time on the last lap, as the person entering the stadium section first usually goes on to win. 'Even if it means crashing, I am going to brake later than him,' I thought. Sure enough, I squeezed up his inside and won the race. I was on top of the world again.

The photographer told me to 'give it some', so my celebration does look a bit staged.

Has Slight got alopecia on one side of his head?
No, it's just his new hairstyle!

Hockenheim

Climbing over the front of the bike,
trying to keep the front wheel down
while right on the limit. I am wearing a
breathing strip on my nose, but I soon
got rid of it as it flapped around and
was very distracting.

Danielle,
my motivation
for winning the race

Monza

Monza is very similar to Hockenheim, in that it is a very fast circuit, and one that I enjoyed. It can be dangerous, when two or three bikes are drafting each other so close together, but fast circuits make for close racing. The leaders slip-streamed and passed each other throughout most of the first race but I seemed able to out-brake the others so, even if as many as six bikes were in the leading pack with one or two riders coming past quite regularly, I very rarely dropped below third. On the penultimate lap nobody came past me. My board said +1.5, meaning I had a decent lead going into that last lap and was able to win by a good margin for that circuit.

I should have won the second race as I had Slight lined up for a drafting manoeuvre but Chili came up my inside and nearly shunted me off the track, causing me to pick my bike up. Even so, we all went over the line side-by-side but that loss of momentum meant I came in third.

I could never stand talking through my helmet during qualifying, as it only took a second to remove it and put it back on again. I am so deep in thought here that my eyes look ready to pop out of my head.

Assen

After double wins in 93, 94 and 95, the pressure was on to defend that record. I had been unlucky in previous rounds, so I badly wanted to get back to winning. On the Thursday before the race I announced that I was going back to Ducati as I wanted to quash all the rumours. So I had even more incentive to prove the people wrong who said that my decision was because I could not win on the Honda any more.

I actually entered the round with two broken ribs from a qualifying crash at the previous round in Japan. It meant that I was really struggling to pull the bike over from the right and into the final left-hand corner, but I still managed to break away and win the first race quite comfortably after an early battle with Kocinski, Chili and Corser. Even though it was close, the other riders and especially Chili would hold me up and so I always quickly regained the lead. In the second race I was neck-and-neck with Kocinski entering the final chicane. He was good through there and it was only in later years that I improved through that section. I was leading, though, and braked as late as I could. Even so, he came underneath me but ran wide. So I flicked it back into first, when I would usually have been in second, and squared the corner off. Corser had come through as well and you could have thrown a blanket over the three of us on the line. But I had clinched it to become the first Honda rider to record a double win. That was one of the best races I had ever won and I celebrated by jumping up and down on the bike like a monkey.

Ready to leave the garage. Slight might have been out on his spare bike as there is one in the background without a tyre in.

Just about to glance across at my pit board while going through start-finish. Normally, I used to look big on a bike but that bodywork made me look tiny.

The final bend of the second race. Kocinski was on the inside of me but couldn't get it back for the final corner.

Assen

Entering the final chicane in the early stages of the second race. Corser is on my back wheel, watched by the usual massive Assen crowd.

Chili looks like George Michael and Slight has come up with another of his hideous hair-dos for the first race podium. I always tried to hold my Michelin cap so that their logo could be seen while the national anthem was playing

Clutching the massive trophy, which is still the first one you see as you enter my house, while being interviewed by the world and their mums.

Donington

This was my 40th World Superbike victory and my first back on a Ducati after my year with Honda. I was happy because Slick was now back in my team but the team was still pretty disorganized under the leadership of Virginio Ferrari.

We had started off testing the 1996 bike and while the new model had more power, I found I couldn't put that power down effectively on the track. In the first race I had led until about two laps from the end, when Slight overtook me. But I hadn't been happy with my set-up and went for a different tyre in the second race, which helped with mid-corner grip. Having passed Chili and my team-mate Neil Hodgson, I pulled away to win the second race quite comfortably. Kocinski had been a few points in front going into the round but struggled in the dry and so I managed to leap-frog over him to take the lead of the championship by around 20 points.

A rogues' gallery shot, taken for a Sky Sport advert.
I think it was intended to signify the biggest names in the
sport: myself, Aaron Slight, Colin Edwards and John Kocinski.

Exiting the chicane, in front of Hodgson and Chili, all at different stages of peeling into the corner.

This was perhaps the first time I carried the St George Cross around, not the Union Jack, and my arm was killing me as it was massive!

The four fingers signalled my 40th World Superbike win. This was the only year I had an English flag on my leathers. With hindsight it was a bit too in-your-face, especially as I had it on my helmet as well.

Donington

Hockenheim

Hockenheim

I don't like this circuit, with its horrible long straights. It can be pretty dangerous when you are doing 190mph, an inch off the back wheel of the guy in front. But this race continued my run of wins there and it was a bit more special because it was at the fastest circuit and I wasn't on the fastest bike. It was a fantastic feeling to extend my championship lead in front of a very good crowd, probably the second best-attended for Brits next to Assen. I had been fourth in the first race, with a clutch problem that meant I lost the tow from the leading group.

Switching bikes for the second race, I won by stuffing my team-mate Hodgson up the inside coming into the stadium section. He ran off into the gravel. I was constantly fighting to stay with the main group as I knew that I had to be in the right place at the right time on the last lap. I was! Akira Yanagawa, on a factory Kawasaki that was one of the fastest bikes out there, came second. He was never aggressive enough to get the best out of his machine and would hardly ever out-brake anyone. James Whitham profited from the Hodgson incident to come third – his best result on a Suzuki. When I couldn't understand why Hodgson's bike was faster than mine the team did some tests at the factory and found that it had one bhp more, even though his was much faster through the speed trap.

In the back of the pace car, celebrating with James Whitham. The girl in the car couldn't have been that nice if we were pointing at people in the crowd.

Typical slip-streaming action at Hockenheim, with Scott Russell leading, me behind, and then Chili and Hodgson

The start of the race and I must have qualified on the second row, because I usually made better starts than this (fourth from right). But I might have easily come out of that first corner in the lead as I was less cautious than most, braking as late as possible at the start of the race. I was always a good starter, even from my schoolboy motocross days. Some riders keep a constant rev from the throttle on the line, but I used to blip it.

Hockenheim

Brands Hatch

If there was one track that I really wanted to win at, it was always Brands. And I would have won both races had the first not been stopped, when Graeme Ritchie was killed in an accident. I had been in the lead but crashed after the restart when, impatient at being held up by Hodgson and Kocinski in front, I was too hard on the gas coming out of Druids. The rear end came round and I almost managed to control it before the front end went, and I took Crafar down with me. The second race was also stopped, due to rain, but I had built up a four-second lead over Kocinski, despite Chili having crashed out when my bar touched the back of his bike as I claimed the lead by going underneath him. Local wild card Michael Rutter cleared off in the restarted race but I was able to stay with Kocinski in the wet, even getting my knee down on occasions, which was unusual for me in those conditions. But I had missed out on a double win and started to get the feeling that it wasn't going to be my year.

The start of the second lap of the first race, with the huge crowd in the background watching me lead the rest.

A1 Ring

After Brands I was just seven points behind Kocinski but I had to work my socks off for my wins. And the next race in Australia was no different. I never really felt at home on the Ducati all that year. At the A1 Ring circuit, I was riding on the limit and getting away with it again. I lost the lead on every straight but more often than not re-took it on the brakes. On the final lap I went back to the front at the tight hairpin and managed to hold on. I was also leading the second race until I noticed a few spots of rain on my visor and was in two minds whether to go for broke or to back off a little. Kocinski seized his chance and took me. I went mental. And, for the only time in my career, I tried to knock another rider off his bike. He knew I would out-brake him at the slow hairpin, so he braked later than normal. And I was even later still. But I hesitated for a second and, instead of letting go of the brake and running through, which probably would have meant him crashing but me staying upright, I ran into the back of him. He wobbled through the gravel and I went down. It was going to be his year not mine.

The battle of the second race, in which I tried to knock Kocinski off. I lead him going into the hairpin and am again struggling to keep the power down.

Assen

This has to be the most embarrassing reason for not winning a race. Kocinski was a brilliant rider but a freak of nature. He had a phobia about cleanliness and thus did not fit in with any of his teams. But he became stronger as the year progressed, whereas we seemed to weaken.

I had led in the first race until the final lap, when he came past me. But I was confident that I was quicker than him through the chicane and I would be able to retake the lead before entering the final straight. That was until a massive bluebottle splattered all over my visor and I couldn't see a thing. After all the problems with the bike that year I knew I would be a laughing stock if I used that excuse, so only Slick knew the real reason.

I was really down between races and Frankie Chili told me to concentrate on beating him in the second race. I told Slick to put the difference between Kocinski and me up on my board and, despite dropping from +6 at one stage to +3, I was able to maintain that margin on Kocinski. So when I entered the final chicane it was actually with Chili behind me, and I had to work hard to hold him off.

In the battle of the second race, I'm holding off Chili in the final stages.

Sentul

The only thing at stake here really was second place in the championship as Kocinski had already won the title, while Slight was only seven points behind me in third. But amazingly, Kocinski did not help his team-mate in the first race, only allowing Slight to finish second behind him, while I came third. There was a bit of a showdown in the Honda camp over lunch, which was very amusing. My win in the second race, which clinched second place, was probably my luckiest ever. Kocinski (who had had more than his fair share of luck throughout the year) tried to overtake Crafar going into a corner from about four miles back. Crafar broke his collarbone in the crash. Kocinski went down with him, the first race he hadn't finished that year, while I then picked my way through the debris to win the race.

Sentul wasn't a good place to crash. You never knew what kinds of snakes or lizards were lurking in the in-field. After celebrating on the rostrum I went into Crafar's garage and gave the trophy to one of his mechanics and said 'Simon won that, not me.' I wasn't in the mood for the end-of-season celebrations in Jakarta that night!

These two Japanese guys, Noriyuki Haga and Akira Yanagawa, who should have been used to the heat, look as knackered as I am.

Phillip Island

Phillip Island

This was the first race of a big year for me. I had undergone knee surgery during the winter to repair a torn ligament and was suffering with motivational problems after a frustrating return to Ducati the previous year. But I now had a new boss and, where others might have left me alone, Davide Tardozzi told me in no uncertain terms that he expected me to win the title again.

It was stinking hot and blowing a gale for the first race. They were the windiest conditions I have ever raced in and my face was as red as a beetroot by the time I finished. In only the second corner of the race I was blown off line and lost two places, but I fought my way back to the front and eventually pulled away. I was more surprised than anyone to start with a win because my knee was still giving me trouble and we had gambled on which tyre to use. In the end, I only won by a second or so, as great chunks were coming out of the tyre; if the race had lasted another lap, I would have had to pull in. There were more tyre problems in the second race as, after getting into the lead, the rear started to chatter badly and all I could manage was third. Even so, I left Australia leading the championship along with Haga.

My body position here shows how I'm trying to keep the bike down while getting on the power and trying to change direction.

Albacete

I entered this round eight points behind Haga and my prospects didn't improve when I crashed out on my Superpole out-lap. The bike shaved a big bit of skin off my little toe, which took weeks to heal. Then, in a wet first race, I was gutted when I finished ninth. But then the sun came out and dried the track and I got a great start to the second race from the second row of the grid. I led into the first corner, fully expecting someone to come past me, but nobody did. After a few laps the board said +1.5 so I decided to just get my head down and push on. This round was typical of a very inconsistent year. I had led the championship after the first round but didn't lead again until after the final race of the year! It was a good job that everyone else was just as inconsistent.

Being pulled from pillar to post
as I am dragged away from
the rostrum.

You can see that my eyes have really puffed up while acknowledging the crowd after the second race. That was probably because I'd had my visor open during the wet first race.

Albacete

Hodgson is behind me, peeling into the left-hander at the back of the pits, on the first lap of the second race. He was only ever that close in the early stages of the race.

Hard on the throttle through one of
Albacete's faster sections

Assen

This was the scene of the famous showdown with Chili. Both Troy and I were convinced that he was getting preferential treatment from Ducati that year. He was 10kmh faster than I was through the speed trap and could pull past me down the straights like I was standing still. Although in the first race I was confident I could get him back, I made a mistake at the kinks and lost tow. But there was no way that that was going to happen again in the second race.

Chili and I cleared off at the front and, as we came out onto the back straight on the final lap, I moved across to the left so that he wouldn't get any slipstream. He passed me later after I made a mistake with a gear change but I knew I was faster into the last corner chicane. Sure enough, I out-braked him so now I was first into the straight and was sure to win the race. I had no idea that he had panicked and gone down. All hell broke loose and he started accusing me of trying to knock him off. He was trying to get at me, while I just did a provocative burn-out in his face. And there were more words in the press conference later. On the eve of the next round in Japan he was still threatening to knock me off, even though he was as quiet as a mouse at the actual race.

Celebrating the race win with Slight and Corser. Notice that I have left my gloves on in case I bump into Chili!

Assen

Going, going, gone! Chili's famous crash, which led to mayhem in the paddock

Kyalami

I just knew that 1999 was going to be a repeat of 1995. Having won the title the previous year, despite all my problems with motivation, I was determined to fly out of the blocks and do the number one plate proud. I was going to kick some ass! I was a different person that year. I was focused on setting the bike up as best I could in time for Sunday's races, not distracted by the flying laps that the others were putting in during qualifying. I qualified on the front row, after working hard on Superpole during the winter. In fact I almost won the pole position award at the end of the year, but was just pipped into second by Troy. I needed to finish fourth or higher in Japan but only managed fifth. This round set the standard for the rest of the year when I won both races very easily, the first time I had done the double since 1996, and the second race provided my 50th World Superbike win. They were probably two of the easiest races I have ever had – I hardly broke into a sweat! It felt like I was riding on rails and none of the other main contenders – Haga, Corser or Edwards – got anywhere near me.

Changing direction through the really tight last chicane on the first lap, with Slight and Corser behind. It's a slow part of the track, about 40mph, so it didn't hurt when you clipped the blue hosing with your knee or hand.

Coming out of the second corner at the start of the race, I have already got the whole-shot and am away

Screwing my face up after the first race win, looking like I have something sour in my mouth and not the sweet taste of victory!

Kyalami

This must have been in practice as I am keeping
out of the way in case someone is coming through on a
fast lap. If I was leading a race by a long way, I would

Donington

I hadn't won a race in Britain since 1997 and, knowing that I was riding so well, I really wanted to do well on my home circuits this year. But I was struggling with the tyres in the first race. The win appeared easy but it was actually one of my hardest ever because the tyre went off halfway through the race. It felt like riding on marbles but I knew I had to dig in and keep that three-second gap over Slight by riding over the limit. If the gap had dropped to two seconds I would have had to push even harder, but knowing that I now couldn't really respond to any challenge, I might well have crashed out.

There was no other tyre I could choose for the second race so, despite stiffening my suspension, it was impossible for me to stay with Edwards, who had made a more significant improvement between races. Slight and the rest of the Honda boys were saying that the Ducatis had it too easy – but they didn't know just how difficult that win was. There were even suggestions that I had let Edwards win the second race so that people didn't think the Ducatis were far superior machines!

I cannot understand why my leathers looked so scruffy, as I didn't have a crash at that or the previous round and always kept them in mint condition. (Answers on a postcard please!) I am also using a black visor rather than my usual tinted one.

James Whitham

is full of himself on the
grid before the second
race after winning the
Supersport race, watched
by Slick and TV presenter
Suzi Perry. I am smiling,
which is unusual on the grid

Having a laugh with team-mate Troy Corser during the build-up. We got on well as team-mates as we had to work together to get a better tyre package than the quicker Hondas.

The clock says 12:25 so it must have been about halfway through the race. Slick is just about to put the board out to say how far in front I am.

Donington

Monza

This was a fantastic weekend, one of my best in racing – a massive crowd, a boiling hot day and two really good, hard-fought wins. Honda traditionally had a speed advantage at Monza, so there was every chance we were going to get our arses kicked. I felt faster round the bends and through the chicanes than Edwards, who did have an advantage on the straights. I probably got a bit over-cautious at the start of the last lap and was weaving all over the place coming down the back straight as I knew that I would win the race if I entered the last bend in the lead.

Chili was with us on the final lap of the second race and then he made a mistake, which forced me wide and just onto the gravel coming out of one of the chicanes. All I could do was get my head down and I have never been faster through Ascari. I gained on Edwards all the way round the last bend and caught his slipstream just as we were getting on full power. He dived inside to get me out of his slipstream but it opened the line up for me perfectly and I won by half a wheel. It was so close that neither of us knew who had won and Colin just shrugged his shoulders to indicate that he wasn't sure. When a marshal gave me the V sign, I thought that meant second so I started waving solemnly to the crowd. But what he had actually meant was V for victory and so, when I came back to the pits, everyone was going mad. The irony was that that year they had changed the position of the finishing line from the end of the straight to the start. If it had been at the end, Colin would have won.

A rare aerial view from the famous Parabolica section of the Monza circuit.

Early on in the first race, with Edwards just in front of me and Corser exiting the left part of the first chicane.

Going through one of the chicanes with Edwards and Chili in the second race. I seemed to go through chicanes at Monza faster than those at any other circuit.

Deep in thought, probably during qualifying as I struggled to make the second row

Joined on the podium by Ducati chief Frederico Minoli – this was the only time we saw him during the weekend when he turned up to take all the plaudits.

Monza

Nürburgring

Nürburgring

This was the race that I wanted to win more than any other in my career. Hannah, the daughter of a family friend, had drowned in our swimming pool the previous week and her dad had told me to go out and win the race for her. And it really felt as if there was some sort of divine intervention. My Superpole lap, for instance, was incredible. I had pre-qualified in sixth yet managed to set a new fastest lap for the track at 1:38.843, almost a second quicker than anyone else. I remember Valentino Rossi commenting that he did not believe anyone could go so fast around that circuit. In the first race I was lying in third, not able to get in front of Edwards and Chili. But they both went down in oil that had been spilled from an earlier crash at turn one. It was as though all obstacles to my victory had been removed and I controlled the race from there, despite a late scare with a back marker when we clashed fairings and he slid out.

It was probably my most emotional race victory but the mood on the podium was solemn as everybody knew the circumstances behind it. All the hard work had been done in that first race but I was also leading the second by two or three seconds, with just a couple of laps remaining, when I slid off at the hairpin. I managed to get back on to score a couple of points. It was my only race crash all year.

Escaping into the back of the race truck during qualifying. I was never too keen on signing autographs at that time as I wanted to discuss things with my mechanics while they were still fresh in my mind.

Misano

This was always one of Troy's strongest tracks and I arrived with a 45-point lead in the championship after he had closed the gap at the Nürburgring. I also knew that he was quick at the next round of Laguna Seca. If I could beat him at these two, it would effectively see off his challenge. But I had never won at Misano and it was usually a battle to finish on the podium. I was determined to ignore the one-off fast laps that other riders were posting during qualifying and concentrate on the set-up of the bike. I think I even surprised Troy when I qualified in pole position.

I managed to build up a large lead in the first race but then suffered a problem with the electronic gear selector, which meant that I had to change gears manually, so Troy caught me up and passed me on the outside at the end of the long straight. But I left it late on the brakes and managed to come back underneath him and win by less than half a second. My rear tyre had also gone off but we were able to combat that by stiffening the suspension for the second race, which made it one of the easiest wins of the year. Once I made it to the front, I just pulled away and won by a comfortable distance.

I always rode with one finger on the clutch, although I would never use it except when I was going down the gears.

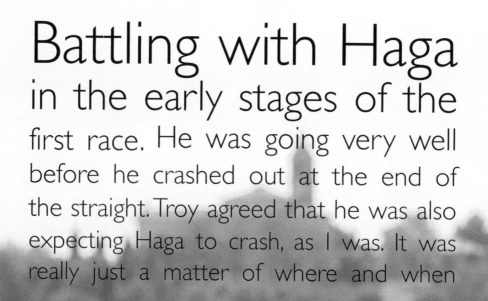

Battling with Haga

in the early stages of the first race. He was going very well before he crashed out at the end of the straight. Troy agreed that he was also expecting Haga to crash, as I was. It was really just a matter of where and when

There are sparks flying off my titanium toe sliders as I put some distance between myself and Troy in front of a big crowd at the first corner.

On the podium with Danielle and Claudia who, at eight and five, were still a little camera shy.

A nice action shot as I pull away to win the second race.

Misano

Assen

I had managed to extend my championship lead at the previous round in Austria, despite only finishing in second and fourth in terrible conditions. And everyone realized that I was going to be very difficult to beat at my favourite circuit. Yet I hadn't done the double there since 1996 and, on a stinking hot weekend and in front of an estimated 60,000 British fans, I didn't want to disappoint.

In both races I was under pressure from Troy in the early stages: in the second race I remember that Troy's pit board said +1.5, then +1, then +0.5 and then +0. Once past him I was able to pull away a second in the next lap and win comfortably. Troy even said after the races: 'There's nothing I can say except that I can't beat Foggy on this track.' Riders don't usually admit such things in public.

The Assen crowd get a taste of the champagne lifestyle.

The usual track invasion at Assen by the British contingent.

Assen

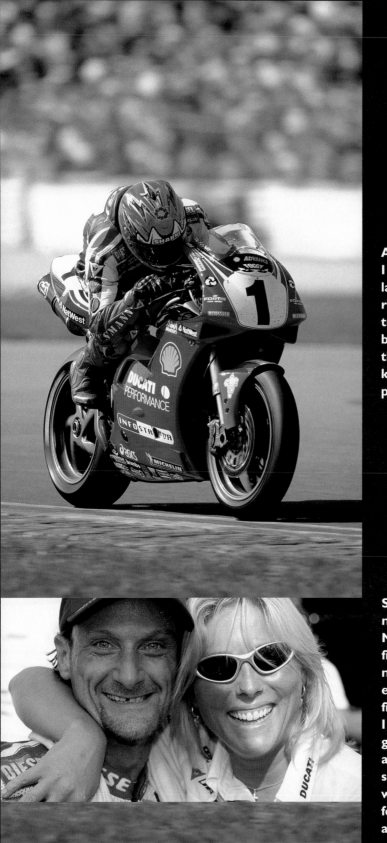

A classic shot: I am exiting the last chicane on the rumble strips, trying to pull the bike back over to the right while keeping the power on.

Sweat is pouring off my forehead as Michaela, as usual, is first to congratulate me. I was never too emotional after the first race because I knew that I had to go and do it all over again. But now the second was out of the way, I was looking forward to a cold beer and a nice big pizza.

Hockenheim

After Assen it was pretty clear that all I had to do was turn up at Hockenheim and stay out of trouble to win the championship and avoid taking the battle to the final round at Sugo. A clutch problem on my Superpole lap meant that I was on the second row but I still got away with the leaders. I found myself undecided as to whether to push for the win or to ride conservatively. But Hockenheim is so fast that you have got to be totally focused, so I told myself to forget the championship and get on with racing.

Unusually for such a fast circuit, as other riders usually draft past you, I was able to stay in front for a few laps. But then I pulled away with Slight and, by the start of the last lap, I was leading and knew that Troy, my main rival, was in ninth. I had won my fourth World Superbike championship. Slight came flying past me, but there was no point dicing with him and crashing out. He was weaving all over the track, expecting me to come back at him, but I was content to pull a huge wheelie as I crossed the line in second, with the world title in the bag.

It was only then that I noticed that Slight was furious and someone came up to me and told me that I had won the race. A red flag on the last lap had meant that finishing positions were allocated from the race positions going into the final lap – and I had been leading.

I am the focus of all the cameras but you can tell from my eyes that I have not been sleeping properly.

Leading Slight, Edwards, Chili and Andy Meklau around the final corner in the second race. Slick has already added 1999 x 4 to my number one.

Hockenheim

A moment to reflect. On top of the Ducati hospitality unit after the races, letting it all sink in while wearing the crown of King Carl, which is still on a statue in our kitchen.

No, Michaela, I won the title – not you!

The whole of the Ducati team join in the celebrations.

World Superbike Statistics 1992

Round 2 – Great Britain   Donington Park 19 April

Race 2

1.	C Fogarty	GB	Ducati	40:48:92 @ 147,86kmh
2.	R Roche	Fra	Ducati	40:51.91
3.	S Russell	USA	Kawasaki	40:51.99
4.	D Polen	USA	Ducati	40:59.08
5.	F Pirovano	Ita	Yamaha	41:02.53
6.	A Slight	NZ	Kawasaki	
7.	R Phillis	Aus	Kawasaki	
8.	G Falappa	Ita	Ducati	
9.	J Reynolds	GB	Kawasaki	
10.	D Amatriain	Spa	Ducati	

Fastest lap: Carl Fogarty   1:37.00

World Superbike Statistics 1993

Round 2 – Spain   Albacete 30 May

Race 1

1.	C Fogarty	GB	Ducati	42:28.310 @135.019kmh *average*
2.	A Slight	NZ	Kawasaki	44:32.103
3.	P Bontempi	Ita	Kawasaki	44:51.377
4.	F Pirovano	Ita	Yamaha	44:51.827
5.	D Amatriain	Spa	Ducati	44.52.219
6.	J Garriga	Spa	Ducati	
7.	T Rymer	GB	Yamaha	
8.	S Crafar	NZ	Ducati	
9.	F Merkel	USA	Yamaha	
10.	R McElnea	GB	Yamaha	

Fastest lap: Aaron Slight   1:34.334

Race 2

1.	C Fogarty	GB	Ducati	44:15.278 @ 134.348
2.	S Russell	USA	Kawasaki	44:18.180
3.	A Slight	NZ	Kawasaki	44:40.960
4.	S Mertens	Bel	Ducati	44:44.207
5.	J Garriga	Spa	Ducati	44.50.380
6.	P Bontempi	Ita	Kawasaki	
7.	F Pirovano	Ita	Yamaha	
8.	S Crafar	NZ	Ducati	
9.	T Rymer	GB	Yamaha	
10.	M Lucchiari	Ita	Ducati	

Fastest lap: Carl Fogarty   1:34.094

Round 6 – Czech Republic   Brno 18 July

Race 1

1.	C Fogarty	GB	Ducati	38:19.36 @ 153.577
2.	S Russell	USA	Kawasaki	38:21.45
3.	A Slight	NZ	Kawasaki	38:34.22
4.	F Pirovano	Ita	Yamaha	38:47.03
5.	G Falappa	Ita	Ducati	38:47.10
6.	M Lucchiari	Ita	Ducati	
7.	P Bontempi	Ita	Kawasaki	
8.	E Weibel	CH	Ducati	
9.	T Rymer	GB	Yamaha	
10.	S Mertens	Bel	Ducati	

Fastest lap: Fogarty   2:06.44

Round 7 – Sweden   Anderstorp 8 August

Race 1

1.	C Fogarty	GB	Ducati	36:28.12 @ 152.31
2.	G Falappa	Ita	Ducati	36:35.42
3.	F Pirovano	Ita	Yamaha	36:35.97
4.	S Russell	USA	Kawasaki	36:36.41
5.	J Whitham	GB	Yamaha	36:36.63
6.	S Mertens	Bel	Ducati	
7.	P Bontempi	Ita	Kawasaki	
8.	A Slight	NZ	Kawasaki	
9.	C Lindholm	Swe	Yamaha	
10.	F Furlan	Ita	Kawasaki	

Fastest lap: Fogarty   1:33.81

Race 2

1.	C Fogarty	GB	Ducati	36:14.17 @ 153.29
2.	S Russell	USA	Kawasaki	36:16.64
3.	G Falappa	Ita	Ducati	36:23.83
4.	F Pirovano	Ita	Yamaha	36:24.16
5.	A Slight	NZ	Kawasaki	36:25.59
6.	S Mertens	Bel	Ducati	
7.	F Furlan	Ita	Kawasaki	
8.	P Bontempi	Ita	Kawasaki	
9.	J de Vries	Nl	Yamaha	
10.	B Morrison	GB	Kawasaki	

Fastest lap: Fogarty   1:33.48

Round 8 – Malaysia   Johor 22 August

Race 1

1.	C Fogarty	GB	Ducati	38:14.21 @ 151.42
2.	S Russell	USA	Kawasaki	38:17.67
3.	F Pirovano	Ita	Yamaha	38:26.36
4.	A Slight	NZ	Kawasaki	38:26.46
5.	S Mertens	Bel	Ducati	36:42.73
6.	P Bontempi	Ita	Kawasaki	
7.	M Lucchiari	Ita	Ducati	
8.	C Lindholm	Swe	Yamaha	
9.	F Merkel	USA	Yamaha	
10.	F Furlan	Ita	Kawasaki	

Fastest lap: Fogarty   1:33.48

Race 2

1.	C Fogarty	GB	Ducati	37:56.40 @ 152.59
2.	S Russell	USA	Kawasaki	37:58.29
3.	F Pirovano	Ita	Yamaha	38:31.57
4.	P Bontempi	Ita	Kawasaki	38:32.38
5.	S Mertens	Bel	Ducati	38:32.52
6.	A Slight	NZ	Kawasaki	
7.	R Phillis	Aus	Kawasaki	
8.	T Rymer	GB	Yamaha	
9.	M Lucchiari	Ita	Ducati	
10.	C Lindholm	Swe	Yamaha	

Fastest lap: Russell   1:30.45

Round 9 – Japan   Sugo 29 August

Race 1

1.	C Fogarty	GB	Ducati	39:06.578 @ 143.347
2.	K Kitagawa	Jap	Kawasaki	39:08.742
3.	S Tsukamoto	Jap	Kawasaki	39:31.362
4.	S Mertens	Bel	Ducati	39:40.629
5.	G Falappa	Ita	Ducati	39:42.991
6.	A Slight	NZ	Kawasaki	
7.	F Pirovano	Ita	Yamaha	
8.	S Russell	USA	Kawasaki	
9.	P Bontempi	Ita	Kawasaki	
10.	T Rymer	GB	Yamaha	

Fastest lap: Kitagawa   1:33.172

Round 10 – Holland   Assen 12 September

Race 1

1.	C Fogarty	GB	Ducati	33:54.78 @ 172.718
2.	S Russell	USA	Kawasaki	33:57.58
3.	A Slight	NZ	Kawasaki	34:22.24
4.	S Mertens	Bel	Ducati	34:22.48
5.	J Whitham	GB	Yamaha	34:26.00
6.	P Bontempi	Ita	Kawasaki	
7.	T Rymer	GB	Yamaha	
8.	A Hofmann	Ger	Kawasaki	
9.	C Lindholm	Swe	Yamaha	
10.	M Lucchiari	Ita	Ducati	

Fastest lap: Russell   2:05.95

Race 2

1.	C Fogarty	GB	Ducati	34:02.08 @ 173.172
2.	S Russell	USA	Kawasaki	34:08.49
3.	S Mertens	Bel	Ducati	34:17.39
4.	F Pirovano	Ita	Yamaha	34:20.86
5.	J Whitham	GB	Yamaha	34:21.19
6.	A Slight	NZ	Kawasaki	
7.	G Falappa	Ita	Ducati	
8.	C Lindholm	Swe	Yamaha	
9.	T Rymer	GB	Yamaha	
10.	P Bontempi	Ita	Kawasaki	

Fastest lap: Fogarty   2:05.75

Round 13 – Portugal   Estoril 17 October

Race 2

1.	C Fogarty	GB	Ducati	41:36.995 @ 143.40
2.	S Russell	USA	Kawasaki	41:45.908
3.	F Pirovano	Ita	Yamaha	41:48.847
4.	G Falappa	Ita	Ducati	41:51.367
5.	A Slight	NZ	Kawasaki	41:51.395
6.	T Rymer	GB	Yamaha	
7.	A Meklau	Aut	Ducati	
8.	B Morrison	GB	Kawasaki	
9.	F Merkel	USA	Yamaha	
10.	P Bontempi	Ita	Kawasaki	

Fastest lap: Fogarty   1:52.186

World Superbike Statistics 1994

Round 1 – Great Britain   Donington Park 2 May

Race 1

1.	C Fogarty	GB	Ducati	40:16.42 @ 149.83
2.	A Slight	NZ	Honda	40:17.75
3.	F Pirovano	Ita	Ducati	40:18.43
4.	S Russell	USA	Kawasaki	40:18.94
5.	G Falappa	Ita	Ducati	40:37.91
6.	S Crafar	NZ	Honda	
7.	P Bontempi	Ita	Kawasaki	
8.	B Morrison	GB	Honda	
9.	D Polen	USA	Honda	
10.	M Moroni	Ita	Kawasaki	

Fastest lap: Corser	1:35.52

Race 2

1.	C Fogarty	GB	Ducati	33:31.787 @ 188.532
2.	A Meklau	Aut	Ducati	33:34.119
3.	D Polen	USA	Honda	33:34.247
4.	A Slight	NZ	Honda	33:38.632
5.	S Mertens	Bel	Ducati	33:39.094
6.	S Crafar	NZ	Honda	
7.	P Casoli	Ita	Yamaha	
8.	J Schmid	Ger	Kawasaki	
9.	P Bontempi	Ita	Kawasaki	
10.	S Foti	Ita	Ducati	

Fastest lap; Fogarty	1:50.769

Round 9 – San Marino   Mugello 25 September

Race 2

1.	C Fogarty	GB	Ducati	39:12.621 @ 160.518
2.	A Slight	NZ	Honda	39:18.743
3.	M Lucchiari	Ita	Ducati	39:23.911
4.	J Whitham	GB	Ducati	39:41.785
5.	F Pirovano	Ita	Ducati	39:41.844
6.	P Bontempi	Ita	Kawasaki	
7.	D Polen	USA	Honda	
8.	J Schmid	Ger	Kawasaki	
9.	S Crafar	NZ	Honda	
10.	M Meregalli	Ita	Yamaha	

Fastest lap: Russell	1:56.305

Round 4 – Spain   Albacete 19 June

Race 1

1.	C Fogarty	GB	Ducati	44:21.492 @ 136.874
2.	A Slight	NZ	Honda	44:30.300
3.	J Whitham	GB	Ducati	44:36.917
4.	P Bontempi	Ita	Kawasaki	44:37.016
5.	T Rymer	GB	Kawasaki	44:46.028
6.	D Polen	USA	Honda	
7.	A Meklau	Aut	Ducati	
8.	S Crafar	NZ	Honda	
9.	S Mertens	Bel	Ducati	
10.	B Morrison	GB	Honda	

Fastest lap: Fogarty	1:33.081

Race 2

1.	C Fogarty	GB	Ducati	44:33.685 @ 136.006
2.	A Slight	NZ	Honda	44:40.657
3.	J Whitham	GB	Ducati	44:51.481
4.	A Meklau	Aut	Ducati	44:52.169
5.	T Rymer	GB	Kawasaki	44:54.814
6.	P Bontempi	Ita	Kawasaki	
7.	D Polen	USA	Honda	
8.	C Cardus	Spa	Ducati	
9.	A Morillas	Fra	Kawasaki	
10.	S Mertens	Bel	Ducati	

Fastest lap: Fogarty	1:33.675

Round 5 – Austria   Zeltweg 17 July

Race 1

1.	C Fogarty	GB	Ducati	33:32.793 @ 188.424
2.	A Meklau	Aut	Ducati	33:35.716
3.	D Polen	USA	Honda	33:35.989
4.	A Slight	NZ	Honda	33:36.291
5.	S Mertens	Bel	Ducati	33:36.506
6.	S Crafar	NZ	Honda	
7.	J Whitham	GB	Ducati	
8.	F Pirovano	Ita	Ducati	
9.	R Panichi	Ita	Ducati	
10.	R Phillis	Aus	Kawasaki	

Fastest lap: Meklau	1:50.408

Round 6 – Indonesia   Sentul 21 August

Race 2

1.	C Fogarty	GB	Ducati	37:01.075 @ 160.685
2.	A Slight	NZ	Honda	37:03.872
3.	S Russell	USA	Kawasaki	37:12.054
4.	J Whitham	GB	Ducati	37:15.794
5.	A Meklau	Aut	Ducati	37:18.527
6.	D Polen	USA	Honda	
7.	T Rymer	GB	Kawasaki	
8.	A Morillas	Fra	Kawasaki	
9.	S Mertens	Bel	Ducati	
10.	S Crafar	NZ	Honda	

Fastest lap: Fogarty	1:28.064

Round 8 – Holland   Assen 11 September

Race 1

1.	C Fogarty	GB	Ducati	34:11.40 @ 169.846
2.	P Casoli	Ita	Yamaha	34:15.21
3.	A Slight	NZ	Honda	34:16.55
4.	T Rymer	GB	Kawasaki	34:17.29
5.	J Whitham	GB	Ducati	34:17.68
6.	S Russell	USA	Kawasaki	
7.	S Crafar	NZ	Honda	
8.	J Schmid	Ger	Kawasaki	
9.	A Meklau	Aut	Ducati	
10.	S Mertens	Bel	Ducati	

Fastest lap: Fogarty	2:06.75

Race 2

1.	C Fogarty	GB	Ducati	34:06.65 @ 170.240
2.	A Slight	NZ	Honda	34:13.30
3.	M Lucchiari	Ita	Ducati	34:14.85
4.	P Casoli	Ita	Yamaha	34:15.09
5.	J Whitham	GB	Ducati	34:16.93
6.	T Rymer	GB	Kawasaki	
7.	S Crafar	NZ	Honda	
8.	J Schmid	Ger	Kawasaki	
9.	S Russell	USA	Kawasaki	
10.	C Lindholm	Swe	Yamaha	

Fastest lap: Fogarty	2:06.40

Round 11 – Australia   Phillip Island 30 October

Race 1

1.	C Fogarty	GB	Ducati	33:50.945 @ 165.543
2.	S Russell	USA	Kawasaki	34:04.703
3.	A Gobert	Aus	Kawasaki	34:05.727
4.	A Slight	NZ	Honda	34:14.661
5.	T Corser	Aus	Ducati	34:21.249
6.	K McCarthy	Aus	Honda	
7.	M Mladin	Aus	Kawasaki	
8.	S Giles	Aus	Ducati	
9.	P Bontempi	Ita	Kawasaki	
10.	S Crafar	NZ	Honda	

Fastest lap: Fogarty	1:35.575

Final Standings
1. Fogarty 305 2. Russell 280 3. Slight 277 4. Polen 158
5. Crafar 153   6. Meklau148

World Superbike Statistics 1995

Round 1 – Germany   Hockenheim 7 May

Race 1

1.	C Fogarty	GB	Ducati	28:48.48 @ 198.044
2.	F Pirovano	Ita	Ducati	28:58.07
3.	J Schmid	Ger	Kawasaki	29:00.12
4.	Y Nagai	Jap	Yamaha	29:00.63
5.	K Kitagawa	Jap	Kawasaki	29:00.85
6.	A Slight	NZ	Honda	
7.	C Edwards	USA	Yamaha	
8.	S Russell	USA	Kawasaki	
9.	S Crafar	NZ	Honda	
10.	T Corser	Aus	Ducati	

Fastest lap: Fogarty	2:02.59

Race 2

1.	C Fogarty	GB	Ducati	28:52.16 @ 197.624
2.	J Schmid	Ger	Kawasaki	28:56.39
3.	A Slight	NZ	Honda	28:56.62
4.	Y Nagai	Jap	Yamaha	28:56.99
5.	C Edwards	USA	Yamaha	29:00.85
6.	S Crafar	NZ	Honda	
7.	M Lucchiari	Ita	Ducati	
8.	T Corser	Aus	Ducati	
9.	P Chili	Ita	Ducati	
10.	S Russell	USA	Kawasaki	

Fastest lap: Fogarty	2:02.61

Round 3 – Great Britain   Donington Park 28 May

Race 1

1.	C Fogarty	GB	Ducati	41:40.53 @ 150.60
2.	T Corser	Aus	Ducati	41:41.53
3.	J Whitham	GB	Ducati	41:53.11
4.	A Slight	NZ	Honda	41:54.01
5.	P Bontempi	Ita	Kawasaki	41:54.19
6.	S Russell	USA	Kawasaki	
7.	J Reyolds	GB	Kawasaki	
8.	S Crafar	NZ	Honda	
9.	M Lucchiari	Ita	Ducati	
10.	A Gobert	Aus	Kawasaki	

Fastest lap: Fogarty		1:35.43

Race 2

1.	C Fogarty	GB	Ducati	41:47.90 @ 150.16
2.	P Chili	Ita	Ducati	41:58.70
3.	A Slight	NZ	Honda	41:59.50
4.	P Bontempi	Ita	Kawasaki	41:59.82
5.	F Pirovano	Ita	Ducati	42:02.19
6.	S Crafar	NZ	Honda	
7.	Y Nagai	Jap	Yamaha	
8.	J Whitham	GB	Ducati	
9.	A Morillas	Fra	Ducati	
10.	M Lucchiari	Ita	Ducati	

Fastest lap: Fogarty		1:35.41

Round 4 – Italy   Monza 18 June

Race 1

1.	C Fogarty	GB	Ducati	32:51.385 @ 190.648
2.	A Slight	NZ	Honda	32:53.332
3.	C Edwards	USA	Yamaha	32:59.357
4.	S Crafar	NZ	Honda	33:02.326
5.	Y Nagai	Jap	Yamaha	33:03.105
6.	M Lucchiari	Ita	Ducati	
7.	P Bontempi	Ita	Kawasaki	
8.	F Pirovano	Ita	Ducati	
9.	J Reyolds	GB	Kawasaki	
10.	G Liverani	Ita	Ducati	

Fastest lap: Fogarty		1:48.330

Round 5 – Spain   Albacete 25 June

Race 2

1.	C Fogarty	GB	Ducati	44:12.784 @ 135.624
2.	P Chili	Ita	Ducati	44:17.543
3.	A Slight	NZ	Honda	44:19.154
4.	F Pirovano	Ita	Ducati	44:19.481
5.	T Corser	Aus	Ducati	44:22.042
6.	Y Nagai	Jap	Yamaha	
7.	A Meklau	Aut	Ducati	
8.	J Reynolds	GB	Kawasaki	
9.	P Casoli	Ita	Yamaha	
10.	S Crafar	NZ	Honda	

Fastest lap: Chili		1:33.779

Round 6 – Austria   Salzburgring 9 July

Race 1

1.	C Fogarty	GB	Ducati	29:43.368 @ 188.433
2.	A Gobert	Aus	Kawasaki	29:48.992
3.	T Corser	Aus	Ducati	29:49.253
4.	A Slight	NZ	Honda	29:49.639
5.	Y Nagai	Jap	Yamaha	29:49.763
6.	A Meklau	Aut	Ducati	
7.	J Schmid	Ger	Kawasaki	
8.	F Pirovano	Ita	Ducati	
9.	C Edwards	USA	Yamaha	
10.	P Bontempi	Ita	Kawasaki	

Fastest lap: Fogarty		1:20.147

Round 8 – Europe   Brands Hatch 6 August

Race 1

1.	C Fogarty	GB	Ducati	37:15.44 @ 168.47
2.	T Corser	Aus	Ducati	37:16.59
3.	A Gobert	Aus	Kawasaki	37:18.30
4.	J Reynolds	GB	Kawasaki	37:19.28
5.	C Edwards	USA	Yamaha	37:19.32
6.	P Chili	Ita	Ducati	
7.	F Pirovano	Ita	Ducati	
8.	S Hislop	GB	Ducati	
9.	A Slight	NZ	Honda	
10.	S Crafar	NZ	Honda	

Fastest lap: Edwards		1:28.34

Race 2

1.	C Fogarty	GB	Ducati	37:13.87 @ 168.59
2.	C Edwards	USA	Yamaha	37:16.80
3.	J Reynolds	GB	Kawasaki	37:17.92
4.	Y Nagai	Jap	Yamaha	37:18.00
5.	A Gobert	Aus	Kawasaki	37:18.21
6.	T Corser	Aus	Ducati	
7.	F Pirovano	Ita	Ducati	
8.	A Slight	NZ	Honda	
9.	S Hislop	GB	Ducati	
10.	S Crafar	NZ	Honda	

Fastest lap: Fogarty		1:28.27

Round 9 – Japan   Sugo 27 August

Race 2

1.	C Fogarty	GB	Ducati	38:32.450 @ 145.463
2.	Y Nagai	Jap	Yamaha	38:37.924
3.	N Fujiwara	Jap	Yamaha	38:45.439
4.	A Slight	NZ	Honda	38:50.002
5.	W Yoshikawa	Jap	Yamaha	38:52.084
6.	K Kitagawa	Jap	Kawasaki	
7.	T Aoki	Jap	Honda	
8.	T Corser	Aus	Ducati	
9.	A Gobert	Aus	Kawasaki	
10.	C Edwards	USA	Yamaha	

Fastest lap: Fogarty		1:31.613

Round 10 – Holland   Assen 10 September

Race 1

1.	C Fogarty	GB	Ducati	33:55.88 @ 171.140
2.	S Crafar	NZ	Honda	33:59.07
3.	T Corser	Aus	Ducati	34:00.43
4.	A Slight	NZ	Honda	34:00.66
5.	M Lucchiari	Ita	Ducati	34:14.35
6.	J Reynolds	GB	Kawasaki	
7.	Y Nagai	Jap	Yamaha	
8.	P Casoli	Ita	Yamaha	
9.	A Gobert	Aus	Kawasaki	
10.	F Pirovano	Ita	Ducati	

Fastest lap: Chili		2:05.94

Race 2

1.	C Fogarty	GB	Ducati	29:38.34 @ 171.434
2.	A Slight	NZ	Honda	29:45.75
3.	J Reynolds	GB	Kawasaki	29:45.98
4.	M Lucchiari	Ita	Ducati	29:52.39
5.	Y Nagai	Jap	Yamaha	29:54.46
6.	C Edwards	USA	Yamaha	
7.	A Gobert	Aus	Kawasaki	
8.	J Schmid	Ger	Kawasaki	
9.	P Bontempi	Ita	Kawasaki	
10.	P Casoli	Ita	Yamaha	

Fastest lap: Fogarty		2:06.21

Round 11 – Indonesia   Sentul 15 October

Race 1

1.	C Fogarty	GB	Ducati	37:16.719 @ 159.54
2.	T Corser	Aus	Ducati	37:22.104
3.	A Slight	NZ	Honda	37:25.353
4.	A Gobert	Aus	Kawasaki	37:36.269
5.	F Pirovano	Ita	Ducati	37:37.695
6.	M Hale	USA	Ducati	
7.	M Lucchiari	Ita	Ducati	
8.	A Meklau	Aut	Ducati	
9.	J Reynolds	GB	Kawasaki	
10.	B Morrison	GB	Ducati	

Fastest lap: Corser		1:28.676

Final Standings
1. Fogarty 478 2. Corser 339 3. Slight 323 4. Gobert 222
5. Nagai 188 6. Crafar 187

World Superbike Statistics 1996
Round 3 – Germany   Hockenheim 12 May

Race 2

1.	C Fogarty	GB	Honda	28:43.77 @ 199.615
2.	A Slight	NZ	Honda	28:44.07
3.	J Kocinski	USA	Ducati	28:44.32
4.	S Crafar	NZ	Kawasaki	28:45.18
5.	C Edwards	USA	Yamaha	28:58.56
6.	P Casoli	Ita	Ducati	
7.	C Lindholm	Swe	Ducati	
8.	M Hale	USA	Ducati	
9.	K McCarthy	Aus	Suzuki	
10.	R Kellenberger	CH	Honda	

Fastest lap: Slight		2:01.59

Round 4 – Italy Monza 16 June

Race 1

1. C Fogarty	GB	Honda	32:30.739 @ 191.669
2. A Slight	NZ	Honda	32:31.389
3. C Edwards	USA	Yamaha	32:31.757
4. P Chili	Ita	Ducati	32:31.760
5. T Corser	Aus	Ducati	32:31.770
6. N Hodgson	GB	Ducati	
7. J Whitham	GB	Yamaha	
8. K McCarthy	Aus	Suzuki	
9. S Crafar	NZ	Kawasaki	
10. C Lindholm	Swe	Ducati	

Fastest lap: Chili	1:47.224

Round 10 – Holland Assen 8 September

Race 1

1. C Fogarty	GB	Honda	33:31.067 @ 173.253
2. P Chili	Ita	Ducati	33:34.107
3. A Slight	NZ	Honda	33:37.001
4. T Corser	Aus	Ducati	33:37.050
5. J Kocinski	USA	Ducati	33:37.256
6. J Whitham	GB	Yamaha	
7. N Hodgson	GB	Ducati	
8. S Crafar	NZ	Kawasaki	
9. C Lindholm	Swe	Ducati	
10. W Yoshikawa	Jap	Yamaha	

Fastest lap: Fogarty	2:04.899

Race 2

1. C Fogarty	GB	Honda	33:32.183 @ 173.156
2. T Corser	Aus	Ducati	33:32.239
3. J Kocinski	USA	Ducati	33:32.253
4. P Chili	Ita	Ducati	33:42.331
5. A Slight	NZ	Honda	33:45.380
6. N Hodgson	GB	Ducati	
7. W Yoshikawa	Jap	Yamaha	
8. S Crafar	NZ	Kawasaki	
9. K McCarthy	Aus	Suzuki	
10. A Meklau	Aut	Ducati	

Fastest lap: Kocinski	2:04.629

World Superbike Statistics 1997
Round 3 – Great Britain Donington Park 4 May

Race 2

1. C Fogarty	GB	Ducati	39:48.996 @ 151.557
2. P Chili	Ita	Ducati	+3.892
3. A Slight	NZ	Honda	+4.137
4. S Crafar	NZ	Kawasaki	+6.380
5. J Kocinski	USA	Honda	+8.215
6. C Edwards	USA	Yamaha	
7. S Russell	USA	Kawasaki	
8. N Mackenzie	GB	Yamaha	
9. N Hodgson	GB	Ducati	
10. J Whitham	GB	Suzuki	

Fastest lap: Fogarty	1:34.637

Round 4 – Germany Hockenheim 8 June

Race 2

1. C Fogarty	GB	Ducati	28:57.410 @ 197.027
2. A Yanagawa	Jap	Kawasaki	+0.697
3. J Whitham	GB	Suzuki	+1.399
4. S Russell	USA	Yamaha	+4.167
5. C Edwards	USA	Yamaha	+4.435
6. S Crafar	NZ	Kawasaki	
7. P Chili	Ita	Ducati	
8. N Hodgson	GB	Ducati	
9. J Schmid	Ger	Kawasaki	
10. A Meklau	Aut	Ducati	

Fastest lap: Fogarty	2:02.587

Round 7 – Europe Brands Hatch 3 August

Race 2

1. C Fogarty	GB	Ducati	39:31.922 @ 158.795
2. J Kocinski	USA	Honda	+4.754
3. M Rutter	GB	Honda	+15.869
4. A Yanagawa	Jap	Kawasaki	+17.488
5. S Russell	USA	Yamaha	+17.499
6. N Hodgson	GB	Ducati	
7. S Crafar	NZ	Kawasaki	
8. A Slight	NZ	Honda	
9. J Whitham	GB	Suzuki	
10. C Walker	GB	Yamaha	

Fastest lap: Fogarty	1:26.366

Round 8 – Austria A1 Ring 17 August

Race 1

1. C Fogarty	GB	Ducati	38:11.804 @ 169.609
2. A Yanagawa	Jap	Kawasaki	+0.297
3. A Slight	NZ	Honda	+0.615
4. P Chili	Ita	Ducati	+1.090
5. J Kocinski	USA	Honda	+1.481
6. S Crafar	NZ	Kawasaki	
7. S Russell	USA	Yamaha	
8. N Hodgson	GB	Ducati	
9. P Bontempi	Ita	Kawasaki	
10. J Whitham	GB	Suzuki	

Fastest lap: Yanagawa	1:30.945

Round 9 – Holland Assen 31 August

Race 2

1. C Fogarty	GB	Ducati	33:31.289 @ 173.233
2. P Chili	Ita	Ducati	+0.931
3. J Kocinski	USA	Honda	+2.988
4. A Slight	NZ	Honda	+4.620
5. N Hodgson	GB	Ducati	+13.426
6. S Crafar	NZ	Kawasaki	
7. A Yanagawa	Jap	Kawasaki	
8. S Russell	USA	Yamaha	
9. C Walker	GB	Yamaha	
10. P Bontempi	Ita	Kawasaki	

Fastest lap: Chili	2:04.649

Round 12 – Indonesia Sentul 12 October

Race 2

1. C Fogarty	GB	Ducati	36:37.726 @ 162.372
2. A Yanagawa	Jap	Kawasaki	+7.767
3. Y Haga	Jap	Yamaha	+7.797
4. A Slight	NZ	Honda	+7.798
5. S Russell	USA	Yamaha	+8.840
6. J Whitham	GB	Yamaha	
7. N Hodgson	GB	Ducati	
8. S Emmett	GB	Ducati	
9. I Jerman	Slo	Kawasaki	
10. M Suzuki	Jap	Ducati	

Fastest lap: Kocinski	1:27.151

World Superbike Statistics 1998
Round 1 – Australia Phillip Island 22 March

Race 2

1. C Fogarty	GB	Ducati	35:38.433 @164.812
2. T Corser	Aus	Ducati	+1.040
3. N Haga	Jap	Yamaha	+3.131
4. P Chili	Ita	Ducati	+9.929
5. A Yanagawa	Jap	Kawasaki	+15.271
6. M Willis	Aus	Suzuki	
7. C Edwards	USA	Honda	
8. N Hodgson	GB	Kawasaki	
9. A Slight	NZ	Honda	
10. S Russell	USA	Yamaha	

Fastest lap: Fogarty	1:35.772

Round 4 – Spain Albacete 24 May

Race 2

1. C Fogarty	GB	Ducati	33:30.118 @ 173.334
2. A Slight	NZ	Honda	+5.278
3. T Corser	Aus	Ducati	+5.425
4. N Haga	Jap	Yamaha	+12.755
5. P Chili	Ita	Ducati	+12.818
6. P Bontempi	Ita	Kawasaki	
7. A Yanagawa	Jap	Kawasaki	
8. P Goddart	Aus	Suzuki	
9. S Russell	USA	Yamaha	
10. J Whitham	GB	Suzuki	

Fastest lap: Fogarty	2:04.554

Round 11 – Holland Assen 6 September

Race 2

1. C Fogarty	GB	Ducati	31:09.535 @ 136.295
2. A Slight	NZ	Honda	+6.032
3. T Corser	Aus	Ducati	+8.807
4. C Edwards	USA	Honda	+15.357
5. J Whitham	GB	Suzuki	+16.162
6. A Yanagawa	Jap	Kawasaki	
7. P Goddart	Aus	Suzuki	
8. N Haga	Jap	Yamaha	
9. N Hodgson	GB	Kawasaki	
10. I Jerman	Slo	Kawasaki	

Fastest lap: Slight	1:32.845

Final Standings
1. Fogarty 351.5 2. Slight 347 3. Corser 328.5 4. Chili 293.5
5. Edwards 279.5 6. Haga 258

World Superbike Statistics 1999
Round 1 – South Africa   Kyalami 28 March

Race 1

1.	C Fogarty	GB	Ducati	43:35.637 @ 146.821
2.	T Corser	Aus	Ducati	+5.257
3.	A Slight	NZ	Honda	+9.779
4.	N Haga	Jap	Yamaha	+13.181
5.	C Edwards	USA	Honda	+14.535
6.	A Yanagawa	Jap	Kawasaki	
7.	P Chili	Ita	Suzuki	
8.	G Lavilla	Spn	Kawasaki	
9.	D Romboni	Ita	Ducati	
10.	R Ulm	Aut	Kawasaki	

Fastest lap: Edwards	1:43.800

Race 2

1.	C Fogarty	GB	Ducati	43.41.963 @ 146.467
2.	A Slight	NZ	Honda	+6.073
3.	T Corser	Aus	Ducati	+7.279
4.	C Edwards	USA	Honda	+12.401
5.	A Yanagawa	Jap	Kawasaki	+15.632
6.	G Lavilla	Spn	Kawasaki	
7.	P Goddard	Aus	Aprilia	
8.	P Chili	Ita	Ducati	
9.	D Romboni	Ita	Ducati	
10.	K Fujiwara	Jap	Suzuki	

Fastest lap: Fogarty	1:43.477

Round 3 – Great Britain   Donington Park 2 May

Race 1

1.	C Fogarty	GB	Ducati	39:19.856 @ 153.391
2.	A Slight	NZ	Honda	+3.430
3.	C Edwards	USA	Honda	+16.483
4.	C Walker	GB	Kawasaki	+20.942
5.	A Yanagawa	Jap	Kawasaki	+21.424
6.	T Corser	Aus	Ducati	
7.	J Reynolds	GB	Ducati	
8.	S Hislop	GB	Kawasaki	
9.	S Emmett	GB	Ducati	
10.	N Haga	Jap	Yamaha	

Fastest lap: Fogarty	1:33.700

Round 5 – Italy   Monza 30 May

Race 1

1.	C Fogarty	GB	Ducati	32:13.009 @ 193.427
2.	C Edwards	USA	Honda	+0.120
3.	P Chili	Ita	Suzuki	+0.547
4.	T Corser	Aus	Ducati	+11.131
5.	A Slight	NZ	Honda	+13.953
6.	N Haga	Jap	Yamaha	
7.	A Yanagawa	Jap	Kawasaki	
8.	G Lavilla	Spn	Kawasaki	
9.	P Goddard	Aus	Aprilia	
10.	A Meklau	Aut	Ducati	

Fastest lap: Corser	1:46.533

Race 2

1.	C Fogarty	GB	Ducati	32:18.285 @ 192.900
2.	C Edwards	USA	Honda	+0.005
3.	P Chili	Ita	Suzuki	+0.544
4.	T Corser	Aus	Ducati	+8.263
5.	A Yanagawa	Jap	Kawasaki	+12.449
6.	N Haga	Jap	Yamaha	
7.	G Lavilla	Spn	Kawasaki	
8.	A Meklau	Aut	Ducati	
9.	K Fujiwara	Jap	Suzuki	
10.	V Guareschi	Ita	Yamaha	

Fastest lap: Chili	1:46.547

Round 6 – Germany   Nürburgring 13 June

Race 1

1.	C Fogarty	GB	Ducati	35:12.037 @ 163.081
2.	A Slight	NZ	Honda	+7.262
3.	T Corser	Aus	Ducati	+30.178
4.	G Lavilla	Spn	Kawasaki	+35.116
5.	P Goddard	Aus	Aprilia	+36.359
6.	K Fujiwara	Jap	Suzuki	
7.	V Guareschi	Ita	Yamaha	
8.	A Meklau	Aut	Ducati	
9.	C Lindholm	Swe	Yamaha	
10.	J Schmid	Ger	Kawasaki	

Fastest lap: Fogarty	1:39.705

Round 7 – San Marino   Misano 27 June

Race 1

1.	C Fogarty	GB	Ducati	39:57.687 @ 152.397
2.	T Corser	Aus	Ducati	+0.126
3.	A Yanagawa	Jap	Kawasaki	+10.935
4.	P Chili	Ita	Suzuki	+16.366
5.	A Slight	NZ	Honda	+20.205
6.	C Edwards	USA	Honda	
7.	G Lavilla	Spn	Kawasaki	
8.	N Haga	Jap	Yamaha	
9.	V Guareschi	Ita	Yamaha	
10.	P Goddard	Aus	Aprilia	

Fastest lap: Slight	1:35.042

Race 2

1.	C Fogarty	GB	Ducati	39:52.554 @ 152.724
2.	T Corser	Aus	Ducati	+6.496
3.	A Yanagawa	Jap	Kawasaki	+10.664
4.	A Slight	NZ	Honda	+17.337
5.	G Lavilla	Spn	Kawasaki	+18.557
6.	P Chili	Ita	Suzuki	
7.	C Edwards	USA	Honda	
8.	V Guareschi	Ita	Yamaha	
9.	K Fujiwara	Jap	Suzuki	
10.	R Ulm	Aut	Kawasaki	

Fastest lap: Corser	1:34.758

Round 11 – Holland   Assen 5 September

Race 1

1.	C Fogarty	GB	Ducati	33:19.369 @ 174.266
2.	T Corser	Aus	Ducati	+4.443
3.	A Slight	NZ	Honda	+5.827
4.	P Chili	Ita	Suzuki	+7.466
5.	C Edwards	USA	Honda	+12.636
6.	A Yanagawa	Jap	Kawasaki	
7.	N Haga	Jap	Yamaha	
8.	A Meklau	Aut	Ducati	
9.	G Lavilla	Spn	Kawasaki	
10.	C Walker	GB	Kawasaki	

Fastest lap: Fogarty	2:03.914

Race 2

1.	C Fogarty	GB	Ducati	33:22.315 @ 174.010
2.	T Corser	Aus	Ducati	+6.319
3.	A Slight	NZ	Honda	+14.592
4.	A Yanagawa	Jap	Kawasaki	+14.645
5.	C Edwards	USA	Honda	+14.771
6.	P Chili	Ita	Suzuki	
7.	G Lavilla	Spn	Kawasaki	
8.	N Haga	Jap	Yamaha	
9.	A Meklau	Aut	Ducati	
10.	C Walker	GB	Kawasaki	

Fastest lap: Fogarty	2:04.113

Round 12 – Germany   Hockenheim 12 September

Race 1

1.	C Fogarty	GB	Ducati	26:19.818 @ 201.204
2.	A Slight	NZ	Honda	+0.227
3.	A Yanagawa	Jap	Kawasaki	+5.106
4.	C Edwards	USA	Honda	+5.408
5.	N Haga	Jap	Yamaha	+10.198
6.	G Lavilla	Spn	Kawasaki	
7.	K Fujiwara	Jap	Suzuki	
8.	P Goddard	Aus	Aprilia	
9.	I Jerman	Slo	Kawasaki	
10.	V Guareschi	Ita	Yamaha	

Fastest lap: Fogarty	2:00.428

Final Standings
1. Fogarty 489 2. Edwards 361 3. Corser 361 4. Slight 323
5. Yanagawa 308 6. Chili 251